COLLECTED

Poems

I

MICHAEL CREAGAN

Collected Poems I

© 2022 Michael Creagan

ISBN 978-1-66783-978-3

Dedication

For my father and mother; Paul and Catherine
For my brothers and sisters;
Richard, Katy, Tom, David, Ellen and Lori
For my children;
Sara and Rachel,
Sean and Michael,
Michelle, Lindsey, and John

For Bob Mezey, in memoriam
and for Sid

I dream of the perfect book.
The pages are all white.
There is not one word,
only the pure desire
nobody can read.

I might have wanted something else, of course,
but tell me how I could have asked for this.

I am meeting you
on this quiet bridge tonight.
The bridge is language.

TABLE OF CONTENTS

Poems From True Love Stories

Poems From Animals And Other Poems

New Poems, Odds and Ends

After A Line By Donald Justice

The last line, but never used in a poem

Too long, you feel, the walls have kept you in.
And you know the walls. The walls are so thin.
There is a shoreless blackness, deeper than water,
that you have seen all day, that runs forever.
Beautiful leaves float on it in this weather.

You are frightened at the distance you have come
from somewhere, but where you can't remember,
or why it was you left, if it was home.

You remember, long ago, running this fast,
the look of the fields when you were lost.

Going To Iowa

lines written when I was trying to decide whether to stay in medical school or go to the Writer's Workshop in Iowa to write poetry

To go all the way out there for *this*?
Writing poems is a strange business.
I might write of all the things I'd miss,
in Iowa.

Could the land be flatter than what I'd write,
smoking and sweating, late every night,
to find some words that would be all right,
in Iowa?

I'm naturally quiet anyway.
I would be nervous every day,
hanging around with nothing to say,
in Iowa.

October's Child

You will be born soon.

I wait with such desire

and know it is not enough.

There are few words for fathers.

Sometimes I fear there is nothing

I can speak to you ever again,

having already dared

to call you out of Heaven,

to come, darling, come

and burn in this fire.

O may your desire

be equally terrible.

Memories From Childhood: Drinking Fountain

One of the things I remember
is the fountain in the park,
the taste of the cold water
from the brass spigot, the splashing
into the stone basin,
the quiet sound of the drain,
and how wonderful it was
that the water had come miles,
running deep under the city
from the beautiful lakes,
inexhaustible reservoirs
shining far away.

Memories From Childhood:
In The Attic

I wanted to know that everything is important
and nothing can ever be forgotten or lost.
But things I loved would be lost in a place like this
and that was only a small part of it.
Sometimes I would imagine I was a ghost
coming back to remember all these things:
old rifles, uniforms and bridal gowns,
diaries, love letters, fading photographs,
corsages crushed in books, broken violins.

Heart Attack

There is a storm outside.
She thinks of her good father
in the hospital, and weeps.

The way she shudders with the lightning
you might think she was waiting
for the sound of a great heart breaking,

and she tells me that long ago,
safe on the porch from the rain,
she and her father would watch

the lightning and count the seconds
until the thunder came.

Going

Going away from you
into certain nights
brings back this nervousness
I can remember once,
getting out of the water
as night was coming on,
the wind beginning to move
across the skin of the lake
where fish started up like goosepimples.

In The Hospital; Watching People Die

At first I expected them to go in anger,
or fear and trembling maybe, or raving with fever.
But there is no desperate calling on God or the devil
to fetch them one more time from out of trouble,
nor do they seem to be thinking of the Hell or Heaven
our elders warned us of when we were children.
Their hands are quiet and are not reaching at air
for something to hold onto, someone dear.
No, in fact, they seem not at all worried,
only disappointed, and very, very tired.

A Grave Poem For A Gift

You gave me an elephant,
an antique carved in ivory,
a sign, beautifully tiny,
of all we wished it meant.

I could wish it would grow beneath us
and lift us into the air.
On his wide back, we could soar
to the warmest Africas

and let him run or walk
through all love's steamy thickets
until snow fell in the tropics
or we broke his humping back.

But O such heartless giving
if on one ivory key
I should try and pluck someday
the whole tune of our loving.

My memory, out of tune,
unlike an elephant's,
would sorrowfully note what once
was real is dead and gone,

as everything I love
goes, as an elephant dies,
although we know it has
some hidden, priceless grave.

Shark Attack On The Tennis Court

I am playing tennis with my son
who is eight years old and fascinated by sharks.
He wants the game to be a metaphor
for a shark attack. When he slams the ball to my left
and my weak backhand, he yells out something like:
I am the Great White Shark attacking my father
at his weakest point, my saw-like teeth
tearing his flesh to tiny, bloody pieces
which settle slowly to the ocean bottom.
I am really alarmed, but who would believe me
if I said I was hurt by a shark on the tennis court?
We go on playing tennis in the sun.
He slams the ball at me as hard as he can,
his racquet slashing toward me like a fin.

Wounds

1.

Under bandages,
he conceals a terrible wound,
which he uncovers each night, in secret.

It happened long ago.
He no longer remembers why.
His hand goes into it.

When he is satisfied,
new bandages are provided.
The wound must never heal.

2.

One hand in bandages,
the child gathers his friends
so he can tell his story.

He put a needle in,
right into my thumb.
And then he took a knife
and cut away the infection
and the whole fingernail.
This pan was full of blood.
It hurt an awful lot,
but I didn't cry.

The child runs off to play,
the pain almost forgotten,
waving the gauze like a flag
that will set him apart forever.

It is painful to look back.
I am still a child.
There are innumerable wounds,
proud bandages.

Divorce

The safe and beautiful bridges into the future
are blowing up before you can get across.
After the battle, the body count is fiction.
You are trying to get away, with the dead on your back,
and you think you should report yourself as dead,
if only you could remember who you are.
If you have a life at all, it is a story
you tell yourself, always making it up.
Of course, it always was, but now you know it,
and it comes apart at night, in your bad dreams,
in the separate houses, when you fall asleep.

I gave you a crystal ball.
You saw a green field
far away, where something
was living. This frightened me.
I think I have given my life
over to dreams, but when
I looked into the crystal,
I had fallen so low
I could summon none of them,
I could see nothing at all.

Someday, in another life,
finding a photograph,
or a ring, or a lock of hair,
I will remember you
and be surprised into sadness,
but I don't think it will feel
like raking up a severed
hand among the leaves,
though I will be full of questions,
as long ago, as a child,
in one of the huge museums,
when I would stand and look
at the pale, articulate bones,
imagining dinosaurs.

I wish the distance between us
would explain itself,
but nothing will come of it.
It feeds on itself, like someone
who has been hurt very much,
who opens his mouth to speak,
and then remains silent.

It is hard to imagine a landscape
in which this might ever happen,
but I think it would be quiet,
there would be enough light,
and we would be still in love,
neither hurt, nor angry, nor afraid,
but proud of ourselves, our arms
reaching out, our hands
opening like flowers.

No One Should Write About Things Like This

The "Little King" was a character in the comics, long ago,
and I used his name as a term of endearment for my wife,
and sometimes with other things in mind

Bad dreams. The little king
wanted to cut off my head.
She gave me a silver ring.
I was as good as dead.

I ran so far away
I thought I could never come back.
In a dream, I heard her say,
I want to marry Jack.

The ring still hadn't vanished.
But I love you, I said.
I'm back. We're not finished.
I was as good as dead.

She was kind, tolerant,
But I can't give up my life
for something I don't want.
No dream. I've lost my wife.

I'm writing this down alone.
No love. Nobody's home.
Some monsters devour their own.
Some use them for a poem.

On A Night Like Tonight

On a night like tonight, I am trying to enjoy
the life of contemplation, but then I get lost
on one of the dark boulevards of nostalgia,

and end up later in the neighborhood
of fear and despair, where I watch a man without hands
attempting to button his coat against the wind.

The world is ugly and the people are sad
is a thought that comes to mind, and I repeat it,
with delusions of grandeur, with a broken heart.

My wife and children are gone. In the world of action
or the life of contemplation, nothing suffices.

On a night like tonight, I wish I had leukemia.

Wanting To All The Way Down

Out of the blue water

you fall through violet and black

to the blackest, and the light you carry

has nothing to reflect from,

only your own hands

if you bring them close to your face.

The bottom settles beneath you

and will not fall out.

You rise, slowly, to the air,

the bubbly surfaces.

"O This Is The Creature That Does Not Exist"

the title is a line from a sonnet of Rilke's about the unicorn

The world is here and staying all night.

But this is not enough. There is something else

that is always missing.

You think you knew what it was, long ago.

It was forgotten and it went away.

It went away and has forgotten you.

But now it comes so near,

as if just on the other side of a wall

in which a door might suddenly be made to open.

You look outside. Tonight there is a full moon

and the sky is so full of light

it seems almost holy, or unholy.

He or she or it is out there.

It must be so. You want it so much.

On The Literature Of Suicide Notes

They are often found
by the police who state
that the contents will not be disclosed.

It is tempting to assume
that the notes are dangerous,
or even magical,

that they cannot be destroyed,
that the policemen who read them
succumb to a fatal madness,

and that their gifted authors
had been working for years
to finish the impossible,

perfect explanation,
that would leave them with nothing to live for,
that would, in fact, kill them,

since within their own words
they would finally see God.
No one can see him twice.

Fantasy Of The Mad Poet

It is very quiet,
the setting in which I imagine
I write my last poem,
having burned all the others.

I am beginning to die,
composing the perfect note
for a suicide. The poem
will take me effortlessly.

I will not be found,
only my poem. No one
will read it more than once.

In The Museum Of The Mad Poet

This is the room he slept in
and the bed where he made love
with his wife, on the dates engraved
on the small gold plate attached
to the headboard.

These are the glasses he wore
whenever he went out.
The lenses are made of lead.

This is his diary, locked,
with its two entries, written
twenty years apart;

and these, his collected letters
to friends. They were never mailed.
All the pages are blank.

This is the fireplace
in which he revised his poems.

And the poem he wrote the night
he died is in that vault
on the other side of all
the ropes and guards provided
by the state.

The Mad Poet Reconsiders His Position

The white page was once
the holy absolute.
Writing was blasphemous.
Now I think of the page
as simply a blank page
a poem can be written on,
or the page is white noise
that can be tuned into music,
or the fresh sheets of a bed
where something lovely can happen.
This is because I have fallen
in love. I recommend it
for anyone who writes.
It is fun to rescue poems
from oblivion, and name them,
and they do the same for you,
and they wake you up each morning
so you have to make it happen,
and you want to make it happen,
again and again and again.

The Master Sketches The World
One Afternoon

Now he puts his brush
away. The black ink
dries on the white paper.

He has left nothing out
this time, not one spider
or one cloud. A great

wind starts up. The ink
spills across the paper.
Then the sky darkens.

He is taken into the night.

Magical Poem

Night is the sky over this poem.
It is too black for stars.
And do not look for any illumination.
–Donald Justice

A door opens and a man enters the room.
He sits down at his desk and begins to write,
and I do the same, in a room across the street,
Our windows face each other. We wave hello.

I am writing a poem about the sky
that was so strange and beautiful tonight
(such blue shot through with pink as the sun went down)
it cast its magic over everyone.

Let that sky be the sky over this poem.
I've had it with starless nights, portentous moons,
and poems that are always final and sad.
Let that sky be the sky over this poem!

Let it make something truly amazing happen!
The poem is charmed. It is becoming happy.
I am happy and I don't know why.
I look up at my friend across from me

and suddenly we both know what has happened.
We run out into the street and exchange our poems.
We have written the same poem. This is the poem!
We embrace and join hands and begin dancing.

The neighbors come out of their houses and applaud.

Writing Poetry,
After Reading B. F. Skinner

No one knows what goes on in the black box.

The black box is the mind, and all its secrets.

The world goes buzzing by, doctoring it

with positive and negative reinforcers.

I had to write this poem. I deserve no credit.

Mental events are not irrelevant,

but private, like orgasms. You can never see them

and it is useless to talk about them at all

with inaccurate, introspective vocabularies.

All you can see is my hand holding the pen,

my hand moving the pen across the page.

The poem becomes part of the environment.

You can guess what you want, but it doesn't matter,

and I can't tell you any more than this:

I write these poems because it feels so good.

Anatomy Lesson

The anatomy professor
picks up a piece of chalk
and carefully draws on the blackboard
the larynx of a pig.

The larynx of a pig
has the same anatomy
as the larynx of a man.
Then why does the pig not speak?

The pig has nothing to say.

The Problem Of Brain Research

The light he calls his own
may be going out,

but in its own darkness
it keeps on turning and flashing

like an animal chasing its tail,
only more beautiful,

the light wanting to shine
only upon itself.

Hypochondria

Good news. Your electrocardiogram is normal.
The chest X-ray is normal. The blood tests are normal.
That pain in your chest is nothing serious.
But the patient looks at you as if you had slapped him.
Are you trying to say there is nothing wrong with me?

You try again. I am sorry to have to tell you
that your X-ray revealed an incurable lung cancer.
You will suffer a protracted and horribly painful death.
To the family, you say: *There is nothing we can do.*
If he were a dog, it would be kind to shoot him.

His eyes shine, an unhealthy radiance.
The curtain rises on the final act
and he is at center stage, playing the part
that he has been rehearsing all his life.
Now he is happy. Now he has something to live for.

Side Effects

More doctors used to smoke Camels
than any other cigarette.
Kinder to the T zone, indeed.

Think of the children of mothers
who used Thalidomide,

or the workers in plastic factories,
dying of cancer of the liver.

Now spray cans are destroying the ozone layer
and you can start to worry about your own skin.

Fewer men would lose their hair
if all men were castrated before puberty.

Perhaps the occasional use of aspirin
impairs the mind's ability to recall
certain shades of lavender.

Perhaps drinking milk
makes people more philosophic about death.

Do not touch me, friend.
When I am old,
I might remember you
and weep.

Would you really be surprised
if an atmospheric pollutant
made flowers bloom from your fingertips?

What are the side effects of these poems?

Memory

O recreate that hour
Divine Mnemosyne,
When all things to the eye
Their early splendors wore.
-Donald Justice

This prayer runs through my mind while I am attending
a medical convention in San Diego.
From the balcony outside my hotel room, I look across
at hundreds of balconies exactly the same as my own,
at hundreds of gleaming cars in the parking lot,
at a kidney–shaped pool, on the grounds of the grand hotel,
surrounded by grass, by the occasional palm tree.

The hotel reminds me that there are too many people.
The cars remind me of the energy problem
and the problems of mass transit and air pollution.
The swimming pool makes me think of water pollution,
water shortages and kidney diseases.
Palm trees always remind me of French ticklers.

That early splendor depended on ignorance.
When you try to remember, there is too much to forget.

The International Ballroom Dancing Competition

I am sitting in a restaurant with a friend.
I tell how happy I am to be a physician,
how it satisfies all my needs, how I'm never bored.
Then a large group of middle-aged people sit down
at the next table. They sound excited, talking
about the International Ballroom Dancing
Competition. A couple from Venezuela
were utterly fantastic in the rumba.
They have been out dancing tonight, embellishing
their skills in the rumba, the samba, the mambo, the tango,
the foxtrot, the cha cha, the waltz, and God know what.
I try to imagine a ballroom, and all I can think of
is a dim room where a multifaceted ball
of tiny mirrors hangs from the center of the ceiling,
reflecting some colored lights, which gleam also
in the polished surface of a muted trumpet
and a saxophone. I think of diagrams
of black footprints, from Arthur Murray ads.
When I try to think of a rumba, my mind is blank.
I am suddenly depressed, telling my friend
that medicine takes up too much of my goddamn time.
There are so many kinds of human experience
I will never have time for, and in relation to which
I will always remain a complete and utter failure.

Fragment

God is speaking to his psychiatrist:
I want to forget about the universe.
Each morning I create it all again
after blowing it to bits the night before.
Each day I watch what happens, hoping this time
things will turn out differently. But no,
history always ends up repeating itself,
down to the last detail. I have watched this happen
at least a million times. I'm sick of it.
You should see what happens on earth. Late each morning,
the human race appears. I hold my breath.
A short time later, they are dropping bombs on each other.
This is bad enough, but other things
have started to bother me in my old age.
Out of the magical cloud, heavy with promise,
out of creation's egg, always the same
weird characters appear, like recurrent nightmares.
There is an old fakir in India
who charms cobras out of a wicker basket
with a flute. He and the cobra rise up,
eye to eye, their heads swaying together,
and then the fakir suddenly drops his flute
and bites the cobra's head off and spits it out.
Each day I watch this Russian work for years
to write his name on a single human hair.

Each day I listen to a man in France
sing through his anus. And all the insane poets.
Each day I watch my marvelous creation
degenerate into a sideshow. It depresses me.
What do I want to happen? I don't know.
But each day, like clockwork, the wrong things happen.
Always, by afternoon, Beethoven is deaf.
Nixon is always elected president.
It's not funny, I know, but I can't stop laughing.
I appeared to that man in Kansas, the same one,
pretending to be a monster from outer space,
and he was friendly, as usual, and gave me coffee,
but I can't talk to him. And later, as usual,
he went home and shot his wife and kids and the dog.
I was telling my wife last night, their terrible history
is a nightmare from which I'm afraid I will never awaken.
Now I am even beginning to sound like them.
O gods of forgetfulness attend to me
and bless me into a deep and dreamless sleep.

Prose Poem

I meet an old friend on the street and we go into a restaurant. Both of us order coffee. When the waitress brings the coffee, my friend says, "I've changed my mind. I would rather have some tea." The waitress brings the tea and then my friend tells me she didn't really want either coffee or tea. She was only doing her homework for her weekly class in how to be assertive. She says, " I am learning how to be selfish in the good sense. I respect myself. I go to singles bars and start up conversations with strange men and I don't feel compelled to go home with them. In fact, it is fun to say "No" and watch the expression on their faces. We have all kinds of neat exercises to do for homework. I go into restaurants all the time and ask for a glass of water and order nothing else." She laughs. " I also go into a lot of places and ask to use the bathroom. I shop for clothes for hours and never feel any pressure to buy anything. And sometimes I buy clothes with the deliberate intention of bringing them back later. All of this may sound silly, but I really think it has helped me to feel much better about myself. I was finally able to ask my boss for a raise, and I got it. And I'm starting to feel more comfortable about sharing some of my sexual fantasies. With the right people, of course." We finish our coffee and tea. I say I have to go. She pays the check and complains to the man at the cash register that her tea was cold. Outside the restaurant, she asks if she can take me out to dinner tonight, and I say "No," and she smiles at me and I smile back. And perhaps she thinks we are smiling at the little irony present in this exchange, but I think I am smiling because I have been thinking, over and over, throughout this whole conversation: *Someday the sun will burn out.*

The Man With The Biggest
Telephone Bill In The World

He lived alone, but there
was a phone in his room. One night
he read somewhere that *the world*

is an incessant web of signals.
He thought this was probably true
and picked up his phone. He imagined

telephone wires extending
into the night, like a vast
anatomy of nerves.

Each number he dialed would connect him
to someone else. He decided
to call up everybody.

At the end of the first month,
his telephone bill was as thick
as the New York City phone book.

They disconnected his phone,
after calling an ambulance.
Safe in the hospital now,

he sits alone on the sun porch,
dialing the air all day
with his right index finger.

An amazing repertoire
of clicks, rings and dial tones
issues from his throat.

No matter what the other
patients say to him,
he only answers either:

You have the wrong number,
Buddy, or: *If you ever*
try to talk to me

again, I'll call the police.

The Interpretation Of Dreams

In a dream last night, I consulted a neurologist
because of certain problems with perception and thinking.
He examined me, and said I needed surgery
on a small part of my brain in the back of my head.
There had been a small amount of internal bleeding.
It was probably still going on. When I asked what had caused it,
he said he wasn't certain, but he suspected
that someone had come into my bedroom one night,
when I was asleep, and hit me on the head
with a lead pipe. He scheduled me for surgery.

Today I mentioned the dream to a Jungian analyst
who looked embarrassed and muttered something about
the strangeness of dreams in general. I asked my wife
for her interpretation. She only smiled,
and said I should try to figure it out for myself.

Today I met a girl with a scar on her leg.
She told me this story: when she was ten years old,
she was riding her bike on the sidewalk in front of her house
when a plane fell out of the sky and crashed in the street.
A wing brushed her leg as it went past.
She relived this moment often in bad dreams.

Then I read about a man who had fallen from a ladder
and struck his head. He had been perfectly normal,

but after he injured his head, he became clairvoyant.
He thought there was a mechanism for this talent
in everyone's brain, and his accidental fall
had turned it on, like slamming a TV
to make a fine adjustment in the reception.

I have often thought of myself as somehow different.
Once, a complete stranger came up to me
in a hospital cafeteria, and invited me
into a secret circle of magicians and mystics.
He said he could recognize a certain look in my eyes.
I politely declined, but I never forgot what he said.

I remember, a long time ago, waking up
with a really terrible headache. I never have headaches.

I think that someone came into my room one night
and hit me on the head with a lead pipe.

Variations On A Theme

What is beautiful?
This is hard enough,
but Aesthetics will never explain
the sweet lure of the secrets
under Beauty's dress.

I remember a day in the attic
when I was ten years old.
Turning the pages, I found
the black and white illustrations
in the gynecology book.
Perhaps this explains why today,
when I open any book,
I tremble with excitement,
looking for revelations,
rare epiphanies.

The hormones of adolescence
are mind-altering drugs.
I suddenly found myself
in a parked car, one night,
crazy with desire
simply to touch something

which might as well have been
as far away as the moon,
the moon that stared through the windshield
like a policeman's flashlight.

The clitoris is the only
organ in the body
of either sex whose only
function is pure pleasure.

The Book Of Genesis
omits the story of God
dreaming the clitoris.

I am not religious,
but whenever God is described
as a stern and angry father,
I like to think of this.

It is the door to this world.
It causes terrible dreams.
It is Pandora's box
and Eve's seductive apple,
the vagina dentata, the wound

that bleeds with the moon's rhythms,
the wound that never heals.

The darkness we escaped from
we always want to return to.

You are a poem on the tip of my tongue.
I have tried. There is no way to say this.

Dream On A Rainy Day

It is a rainy day,
a good day for sleeping,
I tell myself. The rain
drums me back to sleep.
I have a didactic dream:
I walk out the front door
of my house into the rain,
forgetting my hat and coat
and wearing the unmistakable
look of a fanatic.
I splash along the streets
of old, dark houses,
ignoring my friends who offer
umbrellas and hot coffee.
When I get to the edge of town,
I walk up the face of a mountain,
take off my wet clothes
and enjoy a few minutes
of ceremonial dancing.
The sharp rain whips me
into a fine frenzy,
before a bolt of lightning
introduces me to the crowd.

I am about to begin

a long, general confession
in spontaneous blank verse,
in which I will say out loud
my most secret wish,
the one I am not aware of.
I am saved from all of this
by my wife, who has been patiently
pouring cold water
over my face, saying:
All you do is sleep.
I shudder to think of it.
It is still raining.

So Much Light

The single rose in the vase
is losing its petals fast.
I pick one of them up.
It is not delicate,
but elastic and tough, like skin,
like a severed eyelid.
I knew someone once
who had cut off both of his eyelids
because of love or fear,
or a sense of obligation.
There was suddenly so much light,
he remembered. And there were tears,
but not nearly enough.
His corneas became steamy
with scars, and then opaque.
At noon on the brightest day,
he could only see shadows.
You could see him tapping his way
along the street, terrible
dark clouds in his eyes.
Sometimes he would walk
across the lawns and gardens
and pause to move his fingers,
gently, over the faces
of children, the petals of flowers.

World War II

Grandfather is telling him
war stories again.
He tells him about the night
on the aircraft carrier,
somewhere in the Pacific,
when enemy planes came over.
The lights were all blacked out
on the carrier,
and the radio transmitter
was turned off.
The receiver was still on
and messages could come in.
One plane was flying back
to the carrier.
It called in on the radio,
asking for lights on the runway
and permission to land.
Grandfather was the radio operator,
the men in the lost plane were his friends,
but all he could do was listen.
The plane ran out of fuel
and went down in the water.
"But tell me what they said."
"I can't remember anymore."

The child goes off to bed,
but now he knows what to do
with the broken radio
up in the attic. Tomorrow,
he will turn it on,
and the dusty tubes will glow
with an orange light, and then
he can listen to the silence
after the plane had gone down.

I Am So Happy I Could Die

I would usually tell you
that things are already bad
and steadily getting worse.
But I am happy now
and nothing bothers me.
This happiness has descended
on me like grace. I have done
nothing to deserve it,
and it depends on nothing
that can be taken away.
Tonight I imagine the sky
as the interior of a bell
where the moon swings back and forth
with the rhythm of a heart,
or a slow loving rhythm.
Each time the bell is struck,
the world is created again,
but there is no sound at all,
only this thrill in the bones,
the thrill of being alive
and in love with it. And I think
if the world should end tonight,

the stars fall from the sky,
it would be all right, it would be
like snow in July, another
unexpected blessing.

Soliloquy Of The Birthday Party Magician

I know how the great Houdini
made the elephant vanish
on the stage of the Hippodrome.

I'm happy making coins
and oranges disappear
in front of the amazed

faces of children. For them,
I endure the uncouth rabbits
who often shit in my hat,

and for them I'm sometimes ashamed
of the rubber bands in my sleeves,
the flesh-toned shells on my fingers.

Tired of these illusions,
anyone might wish
for another kind of magic.

I understand why Crowley
entered the magic circle
for his invocations,

and why Houdini looked years
for someone who could tell him
how to escape from death.

I am also afraid of death.
We are like the doves,
trembling, in his pockets.

But Crowley went raving mad,
talking to himself
in the middle of the desert;

and Houdini was disappointed;
always the hands of the spirit
were fashioned out of wax.

It is difficult not to wish
for another kind of magic.
Nonetheless, I'm in love

with the magic that there is.
I have been close to despair,
but I am always amazed.

Rain falls from the sky
and a flower blooms in the dirt.
Women bring forth children

and the sun pulls the world each morning
out of night's black hat,
so I am beside myself

and practice my tricks again,
all my splendid illusions,
my grand metaphors.

I have practiced for so long,
standing in front of my mirrors,
I can almost fool myself.

You should see what I can do
with my silk handkerchiefs,
my mysterious Chinese sticks,

my rings, my magic wands.
I would never tell you
this is not real magic.

The Night Of The UFO Sighting

Last night a farmer reported
that a flying saucer had landed
in the woods next to his barn.
Hundreds of people came
and helped the local police
explore the woods, hoping
to discover the flying saucer
or a patch of scorched grass,
or the imprint of a landing pod
in the mud. From the top of a hill,
overlooking the woods,
I could see their flashlights and lanterns
moving back and forth
below me in the darkness.
They found nothing, of course.
I am from outer space.
I am a million years old.
There are no flying saucers,
but I have lived here for years
and I can understand
why they have been dreamed up
by these people, whose small lives
are shadowed by pathos and dread.
I will live forever
and I have my own dreams.

Tonight when I went to bed,
I floated out of my body
over Pennsylvania.
I saw the design of cities
and watched the brain of an ant.
I saw all the bones in the earth
and the bones above the earth,
buried in flesh. I watched
what happens when a man dies.
I saw a man and a woman
making love, and I heard
what they promised each other tonight,
and could see how the promises would be
broken. I could hear,
deep in the bodies of women,
the quiet sound of conception.
I saw the sleeping faces
of children. The air was thick
with dreams. I understood
the past and future explained
in this one night. I saw things
I cannot explain in this language.
Flocks of birds went by
with moonlight on their wings,
and the full moon was reflected

in a thousand lakes.
It was all so beautiful,
and it was almost enough,
but when I went out to the woods
tonight, I wanted to see
a flying saucer, or I wanted
something unimaginable
to happen, and it never does.

The Brilliant Room

You are escorted into
the brilliant room to wait
for the person with the answers.

You are going to find out why
you had an unhappy childhood,
why your marriage failed.

Finally you will hear
the answers to all of the old
enigmas, including your favorite:

*Why is there something and not
nothing?* Here comes the person
with all the answers. What happens

next is pure chaos.
Suddenly you are exhorted
in millions of languages

no one has ever heard of,
though you think you recognize
some phrases of Latin and Greek.

In spite of yourself, you laugh,
you weep, you begin to dance
and sing. But after a while,

you realize there is unlimited
energy here and, after
all, you have your limits.

This is preposterous,
you say to yourself, as you leave
the brilliant room. You hear:

Keep up the good work.

Consultation

The girl blows her nose and tells me:
"Doctor, my nose is running and my throat hurts
and I've been coughing so much
I couldn't get to sleep at all last night.
What do you think I have?"

Christ, this is serious,
I think to myself, thinking of something else,
but she is waiting for my opinion so I tell her:
You have beautiful blue eyes.

Night

The poppies fold their petals when night comes.
I have seen it happen. I am jealous.
I have been trying to close up all night long.

I feel like a service station, somewhere in Kansas,
open all night, where some deluded bastard
thinks he is going to improve himself
by reading the encyclopedia through.

Three blocks away, you are sleeping with someone else.
This peace is not experienced as peaceful.

It is dark. It is beginning to rain.

Looking For Metaphors In The Mountains

These crazy birds, zooming around our heads,
almost as quick as thoughts, could be our thoughts,
and so could the monstrous shadows of the clouds,
coming, like patches of night, across the mountains.
And the bushes of flowers by the fire road
could be your dreams, dreams I want for you
when you remember this, when you are gone,
dreams that bloom all night like wildflowers.
Even here in the desert, here on this mountain,
they conjure blossoms out of earth and water,
blossoms of pink and white and blue and gold.
And no one comes to gather flowers here,
but still they labor to be beautiful,
or more amazing, labor not at all,
but simply *are* like this, like a burning bush
or quiet fireworks, Roman candles
always exploding, never coming down.

Long Distance

There is a shell,
an imaginary shell,
convoluted, pale,
all in my mind,
and it *is* my mind.
When I listen,
there is a sound
like the sound that a shell makes
when you hold it close to your ear.
It is not the sound
of the Pacific,
or the sound of my own blood,
but a voice,
that must be your voice,
whispering, deep
in the pink interior.

This is how you teach me this poem.
This is why I stay up all night,
writing it down for you.

Why I Dropped Everything
And Drove To Maine

Wyoming was beautiful.

Nebraska was a bitch.

The country went by like this,

and there I was in Maine,

with a sheepish smile on my face.

I had driven three thousand miles

to give this woman a kiss,

like the last foolish romantic,

and proud of it, of course.

The Foolish Romantic Has A Vision

Huge crates of china
and linen and silver and crystal
are sinking into the lake.

The bride surfaces
on the back of a white horse,
who gallops out of the water
and heads for the distant hills,
after dropping a note at my feet.

It is a form letter.
To Whom It May Concern:
You were born to love this woman.
I am taking her far away.
I am not coming back.

I throw myself into the water
and begin to calm down.
I have always been sad.
Now I know why.
This begins to make me happy.
I forget how to drown.

Poem For Pamela Solar Mills

Your name suggests a place
where sunlight is manufactured,
and I think that is perfect,
because when I told you today
that eyes were created by sunlight,
I was really thinking of you,
and how, because of you,
there was nothing I could do
except to learn to be glad
and see visions, and write
these crazy poems to explain them.

Post Coitum Omne Animal Triste Est

No sadness should follow this,
but no matter where I look
I can see that you are missing,
my cock seems ridiculous
taken out of context,
and I feel lost in this bed
with only your name in my mouth,
my hands incredibly empty.

Snowy Night One Year From Now

It is a year from now.
Pamela is standing
in a pale circle of light,
on a snowy street,
a street I have never seen,
in Amherst, Massachusetts.
She is waiting for someone.
It seems as if the snow
has been coming down for years
and will keep on falling,
and the person she is expecting
will never arrive. The night
is like a ball of glass
in which you can watch the snow
falling softly forever
into the perfect stillness
of a scene such as this,
where nothing can ever change.
You hold it in your hand.
You are excluded forever.

I will never arrive
to touch Pamela
in the pale circle of light
on a street I have never seen.

But it is not easy
to look away. The snow
catches fire, like stars,
in the dark sky of her hair.

Love Letter

After I learned the language,
I wanted to say something else,
but couldn't think of it.

After the masked ball,
I wanted to take off my face,
but I was stuck with it.

Believe me.
I am not the mad poet,
I am not the foolish romantic.

I am Michael.
I want to tell you I love you
in a language nobody knows.

Moonlight

Perhaps only the moonlight
remembers tonight

the secret path
into the dark woods,

the gold rings that are lost,
that shine under the surface
of forgotten lakes,

the silent attics,
the broken violins,

the empty cages
in the zoos of your childhood,

the overgrown outfields
of deserted stadiums,

the slow orbiting
of abandoned spaceships.

Confessions

I was a pole- vaulter.
I am afraid of heights.

I played the clarinet,
but could never read music.

On my wedding night,
I dreamed of someone else.

I think of myself as a writer.
I love the white page.

Someday I will be dead.
I want to live forever.

Taking A Walk On Sunday

Today we walked through the quiet streets of Claremont
and the sunlit, park-like grounds of the colleges
with their wide lawns and monumental trees.
Over our heads was a sky of the clearest blue,
like the clear blue sky of the mind over the page,
and as we walked, with the sunlight warm on our skin,
it was easy, for once, to feel important and good,
as if we were being read, and understood.

When We Fell In Love

When we fell in love, we thought we had found a way
to understand history, and our own biographies.
Afterwards, we were perplexed, but no more than usual.

The lovers come together and kiss
for the first time, then for the last time.
We were the lovers, not believing it.
Where in these events would you locate the most sadness?

I think of the way a friend described his marriage:
A thousand and one nights of mercy fucks.

Sure, life can be dull,
but some mornings you wake up happy
for no reason at all,
or a tree you thought was dead
blossoms overnight,
suddenly beautiful,
and still the future stretches out
to the cloudbank of oblivion on the horizon
like a minefield of pleasant surprises,
an occasional triumph of hope
over experience.
Which is why we want to live forever.

And still somewhere inside you
is the child running in circles,
feeling for the first time what it's like
to think about *forever*
and *never again.*

Anosmia

If you're legally blind, you can carry a white cane.

If you lose your sense of smell, who gives a damn?

I lost my sense of smell twelve years ago

after three operations on my nose

to remove nasal polyps. Now I can breathe,

but my mucous membranes are scarred and respond to
nothing.

Millions of molecules bounce off their hard walls,

but no lights come on in my olfactory lobes.

I live now in Claremont, California.

Flowers are everywhere, and citrus trees,

but I walk down the beautiful, blooming streets

amusing myself by recalling the fond memory

of my last aroma, in 1966:

a trash can, under a fire escape, in Pittsburgh.

My Mother And Father

My mother and father are walking through Edgewood Park
the night before their wedding, a night in June,
in New Haven, in 1943.
Walking behind them is my Aunt Loretta,
my father's maiden aunt from Illinois,
a silent, uninvited chaperone.
She explained to my angry mother after the wedding
she had wanted my parents to have no chance that night
to do anything they might regret later,
regret for all the rest of their married lives.
My mother has never forgiven her for this.
My father thinks it was none of her business
but *her heart was probably in the right place.*

Forty years later, I drive by Edgewood Park
on an autumn visit to Connecticut.
An October evening, and the lights of New Haven are on,
but the park looms in the middle of the city
like a black forest. When I was a child,
it seemed the sun was always shining down
on the playground, the woods and meadows, the little duck pond,
so it feels strange to see the park like this,
dark and forbidding, abandoned for the night.
The park was my enchanted forest once.

And for my parents, it must have been enchanted
as they walked through the park the night before their wedding.

My mother and father are walking through Edgewood Park,
the night before their wedding, a night in June,
in New Haven, in 1943.

The bright glare of sunlight has softened to dusk
and the air is rich with the scent of earth and flowers
as they walk together down the wide dirt path.
They stop in the shadows of a giant elm
to kiss each other, then continue down the path,
holding hands, talking, laughing a little,
once in a while looking up at the sky
where the moon and stars are becoming visible,
once in a while looking over their shoulders
at Aunt Loretta. Perhaps they both are dreaming
of their wedding night, perhaps they are dreaming
of the children they will love together,
perhaps they are both dreaming about me.
As they walk along the path, now silvered with moonlight
and vanishing up ahead in the dark shadows,
do they think they will always be in love like this?
Of course they do, but that is another story.
This is how I like to imagine them
at the beginning of their love story

before the acid of time could start its work.
But they are still together, and still in love.

And I have been driving in circles around New Haven,
dreaming about the world before I was born
and wondering how the powers of luck and love
can conjure someone out of oblivion
to *the million-petalled flower of being here.*
But here I am, feeling lucky and loved,
in a world as full of mystery as ever.
I doubt that anyone walks through the park tonight.
It's a cold night, and rain is starting to fall,
and I turn on the windshield wipers, and drive on.

Wolves

My wife had been afraid of wolves since childhood
when she had recurring dreams of the same wolf
who would wait outside her window, night after night,
howling and drooling. She would wake up screaming
and her mother and father would tell her the wolf was gone,
but even when she was awake, she knew he was there.
When we went to the Pittsburgh Zoo, I could feel her tremble
as we walked past the wolves pacing in their cages.
I saw a wolf who was standing still in his cage
and thought that he was staring at my wife.

In the fourth year of our marriage, for a birthday present,
someone had sent my name to one of those places
that will investigate your family tree
and prepare an official-looking document
with the crest and shield of your distant ancestors.
I was home with my wife when these treasures arrived in the
mail,
and we opened the large envelope together.
On my family's shield, the heraldic beast was a wolf.

I was frightened, angry and sad, and felt as if
the old familiar world had blown away
and I was standing in another world
where I could imagine the old engines of fate
whirring and clanking somewhere, out of sight.

Slowly the world came back, and we were in it,
however lost. We didn't say very much.
I think we both felt sorry for each other,
and I think that both of us knew our marriage was over.

Valentine's Day

When I was ten, I wanted to give my father
a valentine that I had made at school;
a big red heart pasted on white paper
on which I had written the words: Dad, I love you.
I was too shy to give him the valentine,
so I folded it carefully into a paper airplane
and launched it toward him as he sat in his favorite chair
reading a story to my sister, Ellen.
I watched as the valentine struck him in the forehead
and tumbled into his lap. He picked it up,
not looking at it, and crumpled it into a ball,
then threw it at me, hitting me in the chest,
with a look on his face so angry and unforgiving
that I frightened myself by feeling I didn't love him.
I picked up the valentine and ran to my room,
and lay on my bed, sobbing. My father came in,
and discovered what had happened, and held me tight,
and I held onto him, but couldn't stop crying.

Uncle Pierre

Eighty years old, my great-uncle Pierre
was slowly dying of leukemia
in a hospital in Springfield, Massachusetts.
Aunt Evelyn was with him day and night
because she had been a nurse, because she loved him.
One day she was trying to feed him some rice pudding
but she was nearly blind and, time after time,
she would jab my uncle with spoonfuls of rice pudding
on his forehead, on his nose, or in his eyes.
Soon his face was covered with rice pudding.
"I can't take this anymore," he said,
and then he turned his face to the wall, and died.

For Rachel

I am trying to sleep after a long day
in the hospital. For an hour early this morning,
I tried to resuscitate a six-month old,
a baby boy who was found dead in his crib
when his mother woke up and went to give him his bottle.
This afternoon, in the space of one hour,
three patients arrived in cardiac arrest.
Eventually, I pronounced all of them dead.
I feel as if I'm stained with blood and death,
and I feel as if I want to sleep forever.
When I'm almost asleep, I hear my daughter Rachel
start to cry. I walk into her room
and we get settled in the rocking chair.
She puts her head on my shoulder. I start to sing.
Then I hear the owl outside her window,
the owl that lives in the old cedar tree.
I stop singing, and tell her about the owl,
and she picks her head up, and listens for a while,
then smiles at me, and puts her head back down,
and I go on singing until she falls asleep.

Looking At An Old Photograph With My Four Year Old Daughter, Sara

Sara, where do think you were before you were born?
I was at Baskin-Robbins.

Sara brings me a framed photograph

taken at Christmas, several years ago,

that shows me standing in front of the Christmas tree

with Sean and Michael, Uncle Dick and Jack.

She looks at the picture and asks me, *Where am I?*

I tell her the picture was taken before she was born.

I was just a twinkle in your eye?

I laugh, wondering who might have told her this.

You were just a twinkle in my eye.

But she goes on staring at the photograph

as if she could find herself in her father's eyes.

How certain she is that she was always here,

that she belongs here, that she will always be here.

The Game Of Go

Many years ago,
for Christmas, someone gave me
the ancient game of Go.
This will be fun, I thought.
I liked the stark beauty
of the black and the white stones.

In the instruction booklet,
I found this warning:
The rules for the game of Go
are simple and easy to learn.
However, the game itself
is sufficiently complex
that no one can hope to master it
within his lifetime.

Where did they get this horseshit?
I thought to myself. And then
I played several games
and decided they could be right.

The game has been put away
for years in my study closet,
but still it calls to me,
like the orphans of Viet Nam,
like a career in neurosurgery,
like adultery.

Trying To Stop Smoking

I am trying to stop smoking again
and my sense of personal integrity is gone.
No longer one person, suddenly I'm a crowd.
The man with the iron will appears and dissolves.
The addict picks up the cigarette and lights it.
The connoisseur of fine Turkish tobacco
inhales a lungful of smoke and begins to smile.
The guilty bystander watches all this happen,
wringing his hands, thinking about cancer,
chronic lung disease and heart attacks.
The almost neutral observer writes this down.

Monsters

You might have seen these things
in museums: the child with two heads,
the anencephalic child,
the cyclops. Safe and remote,
they float in glass jars
of pale, discolored fluids.

The child is about to be born
in the delivery room.
The mother has read books
like *Childbirth Without Fear*.
Now she is working hard,
gripping the hand of the father
who is standing beside her.
A camera hangs from his neck.

The child is in my hands.
No one dares to speak.

The woman screams,
Show me my baby!!

We gather around the monster
like a coven of witches,
our mouths shut tight, our eyes
shining with love and fury.

Road Burns

The paramedics bring our patient in.
When we peel off the bloody clothes, we find his tattoos.
Big blue letters across his back spell out
the words: HELLS ANGEL. Across his left forearm,
it says, LETS FUCK; across the right, EAT PUSSY.

He is in his late thirties, losing his hair,
overweight. I think he looks like me.
Give me something for this goddamn pain!
We give him a generous dose of Demerol
and swab Lidocaine over the raw skin.

A nurse gently scrubs his numb wounds with a toothbrush.
"Haven't heard too much from you boys lately."
"No, I guess we've been getting kind of sneaky."
When the nurse is done, he's bandaged with Silvadene
and then sent home with some pills to take for the pain.

We laugh about his tattoos after he's gone.
Looking into his future, I see a man
wearing long sleeves to his daughter's First Communion,
or arriving at a hospital like this one,
after a stroke, perhaps, when he's eighty-one.

When they take the clothes of his decrepit body,
someone will laugh, but also feel uneasy
the way I felt today, looking at him,
thinking about the lives there must have been,
quietly falling apart, under his skin.

There Are A Million Stories

I walk into room A
to see the woman with the injured ribs.
I ask her what happened, and she smiles,
and then she tells me her story:

I work at the newspaper.
This man works next to me.
I've known him for one year
and he seemed very nice, he was always nice to me.
Today when he came to work, he was quiet,
and he looked very unhappy.
So I said, "What's wrong with you?"
He didn't answer. He just glared at me.
Suddenly he slapped the Chinaman in the face
and when the Chinaman tried to hit him back,
he grabbed me so tight I thought he was trying to kill me.
He was standing so close
I could feel his privates against my leg.
They got him off me, finally.
Then he pulled his pants down.
Of course, the Chinaman turned away
because he didn't want to see that.
The police came and took him somewhere.
My ribs were sore, but now they feel OK.
I feel sorry for the man. He just went crazy.
What would make a person act like that?

I shake my head and shrug, as puzzled as she is,
and examine her ribs, and tell her she'll be all right.
She smiles again, she looks very happy,
and I think today is a day she will always remember.
Something strange and frightening happened
but she survived it, she is all right,
and she will tell this story over and over.

I walk into room B
and I see a Chinese man with a bruised face...

After Seeing A Man On Television Who Had Been Struck By Lightning Eleven Times

A good poet is someone who manages, in a lifetime of standing out in thunderstorms, to be struck by lightning five or six times; a dozen or two dozen times and he is great.
-Randall Jarrell

Imagine how it feels
when the sky begins to darken,
and the great cloud-mountains
hammer their kettledrums,
and that old power and light
starts streaking across the heavens
on its long way down,
looking for him again.

Memories From Childhood:
The Night Of The Rosenberg Execution

A hot evening in June. I was nine years old.

My father and I were sitting on the grass

in the backyard, watching the dark shadows

spreading across the lawn as the sun went down.

A Yankee game was on the radio.

Mantle, or Maris, had slammed a long home run,

and I was trying to sound like Mel Allen,

the way he said, *Going, going, gone.*

Suddenly the game was interrupted

by a news bulletin. The announcer said,

Julius and Ethel Rosenberg are dead.

Then he went on to describe the execution.

Julius was led into the death chamber

and strapped into the electric chair.

A heavy black hood was dropped over his head

before the executioner pulled the switch.

Julius was electrocuted first,

and then Ethel, in the same electric chair,

a short time later. Ethel was shocked twice.

When she was examined after the first shock,

the doctor said he could hear her heart still beating.

Later that evening, when I went to bed,

Ozzie and Harriet were on the radio.

I heard their voices, the sound of canned laughter.

My father and mother were in the living room
and their voices sounded faint and far away.
Through the window above my head, I could see the sky.
The moon seemed brighter than a hundred-watt bulb
and clouds were scattered around like soiled rags.
A moth was beating its wings against the screen.
It was a hot night, and I couldn't sleep,
and I lay in the dark for hours, soaked with sweat,
feeling my heart pounding in my chest,
wondering how it had started, how it would stop.

Memories From Childhood: Grandmother

You kept so many together
in your grand old house.
You taught me the clouds and the flowers
and most of my first words.
Now that you are dead
and buried under flowers
I no longer remember the names of,
I can find no words
to bring you back to me.
I am still the child
who followed you down to the cellar
where you shoveled coal in winter
into the big, black furnace.
Standing safely behind you,
blinking against the heat,
I was amazed you were able to keep
such a great fire going.

Recurring Dreams

The first day of school, I am walking home in the rain,
wearing a yellow raincoat. It is dark.
Lights are coming on in all the houses
but I seem to know that all of them are empty.
When I get to my house, I can see it is dark inside.
It looks as if it's been abandoned for years.
The magnolia tree in the front yard is in bloom
and the petals seem to glow with their own light.
The rain falls faster and harder. After a while,
there is only water and darkness and a deep silence
except for a muffled sound like someone's heart.

I am in a rowboat with friends, at night, on a river.
We have stopped rowing, and it is hard to tell
if the boat is moving at all. All we can see
is the moon, and the moonlight shining on the water.
I suddenly see the river disappear
a few yards in front of the boat. I recognize
the sound of water roaring over the falls,
and then the sickening roller-coaster drop
that is like a perfect memory, but of what?

Night School

Here we are again, trying to understand our story
in the calm light of eternity, but shamelessly distracted
by the anthropomorphic clouds, the falling leaves,
and the slow and sexual veronica of August

as it turns into September and October,
the cape swirling around, the future snorting through.
A cloud of dust rises and settles down. Everyone's gone home.
Then there are tears, regrets, hideous handkerchiefs.

A man from Kansas drives out of the Hudson Tunnel
and looks at New York lit up like a monument.
How in the name of Christ did this get here? he wonders,
lost in the stream of history, and bad traffic.

But back to our story, what do you think will happen?
We are always ready to be amazed, we know our struggles
will have an uncertain outcome, but will finally be over,
and no one will survive to remember.

Buried Alive

One cloudy Tuesday, they drove past a cemetery,
and he said to his wife, "Would you like to be buried here?"
It looked like a peaceful place, with its green lawns,
and the grey headstones arranged in careful rows
under the ancient branches of oaks and elms.
"No, I don't want to be buried here," she said.
"I don't want to be buried anywhere. I'm afraid
of being buried alive." He laughed. "It happens,"
she said. "I've read about it. And if I'm dead,
I still don't want to be put under the ground.
I know it's crazy, but it frightens me.
Doesn't it bother you?" He laughed again,
his eyes on the dark road in front of him.
"No," he said, "I'm looking forward to it."

Some Nights

Nothing has happened, nothing is happening,
nothing is going to happen. What do you want?

Some nights your heart feels like a dark ocean,
a calm ocean, dreaming of tidal waves.

Tonight

Tonight I woke up from a dream of pure longing,
a desire I can feel with my whole body,
even now, now that I'm wide awake,
but not a desire for anything I can name.
It feels like gravity, the way I imagine
gravity would feel, as an emotion.
I look out my bedroom window and see the moon,
the full moon shining in a grotto of clouds.
In the fields across from my house, coyotes howl.
Perhaps they are howling their hearts out at the moon,
but who knows what inspires them to howl?
I am quiet, as usual, wanting to understand
why I had this dream, why it woke me up,
and I think that tomorrow, in the hospital,
I will appear to know exactly what I'm doing,
and even feel as if I know, but tonight
I feel lost in this world, and I think the moon
is like the light at the end of a long tunnel.

One Man Walking

One man walking down a country road
with fields on either side, gold and brown.
Off in the distance, hills, and patches of trees.

A day in late summer, or early fall,
a very hot day, the sunlight beating down
from the blue sky, where the clouds haven't moved for hours.

Nothing here tells what year it is,
or where the road comes from, or where it goes,
or why the man is out walking alone

in a scene so calm and still, like a photograph,
it almost seems that time has been escaped from,
and nothing will ever change or ever happen.

A truck roars past, raising a cloud of dust.
The man waves at the truck, but no one waves back.
And the dust hangs in the air a long time.

To A Dear Friend Who Is Living Far Away

After an ancient Chinese poem by Po Chui
For Bob Mezey

Only a year ago, I met a friend,
a master in the art of poetry.
I had been reading his books since I was young,
and many of the poems I knew by heart.
My poems were clearly the work of an apprentice
but he was kind and generous to me
and welcomed me as a fellow in the art.
Many the hours we charmed with talk of verse.
We quoted favorite lines to one another,
often the other's favorites as well.
Some well-loved poems we would recite together
as if we were chanting scripture, or a prayer.
Long ago, a poet friend once asked him,
How many people in the world tonight
are thinking about the meters? We thought about them,
we talked about them. Hell, we reveled in them,
with *the love that masquerades as pure technique.*
I think back often to the night we met
and started talking about poetry.
The doors of Heaven opened in my mind.
I would have laughed, had someone told me then
that after only one brief year had gone,
I would be struggling with how to say farewell

to someone I had simply grown to love

as a father, brother, teacher and dear friend.

Tonight I dreamed that he was back in Claremont

and I saw again the face of a dear friend.

He seemed to be saying that nothing had really changed.

Words can travel at the speed of light

and we will go on talking as before.

I woke up, and thought he was still talking to me.

I turned on the light. There was no one there at all.

On a night like tonight, missing his company,

I will sit at my wooden table under the trees.

A candle will illuminate the page

on which I'll write some words to send to him,

hoping to make him smile, and touch his heart.

Doctor

The nurse's face looks frightened when she tells me
I need to see the patient in Room 1.
I go with her and introduce myself
to the silent man lying on his back,
and remove the bloody towel that hides his face.
Cancer has been eating at his face
and the left side of it is nearly gone,
now little more than an ugly, bloody crater.
He has lost his left eye, part of his nose,
and the left side of his mouth. He opens his eye
and lifts his right hand up in front of it.
He is holding a small mirror in his hand
and stares into the mirror at his face.
He drops his hand, then lifts it up again.
He does this over and over. I take the mirror
and look into the glass, and see my face.
He reaches for the mirror, and I ask him,
"Why do you want to torture yourself this way?"

He smiles at me. I think it is a smile.
"I am not trying to torture myself, Doctor.
I am teaching myself to want to die."
I think of the Latin root of the word Doctor,
an ancient Latin verb that means "to teach."
I think of nothing I can teach this man.

He is teaching *me*, a painful lesson
that he has suffered long to learn by heart.
I want to help. I want to do no harm.
I give him back his mirror, touching his hand,
and watch him lift his hand up to his eye
and go on staring at his ruined face,
the mirror telling the plain and awful truth.

After Reading A Book Of Old Chinese Poetry, I Stay Awake Tonight And Write This Poem

A beautiful place is the town of Lo-Yang.
The big streets are full of spring light.
Wen-Ti, 5th century, CE

A beautiful place is the little town of Claremont.

The quiet streets are lined by ancient trees.

Down the long avenues of old houses,

pepper trees, sycamores, cedars, oaks and elms,

eucalyptus, palms and jacarandas,

translate sunlight into restful shadows.

Flowers are everywhere, and citrus trees.

Lemons and oranges ornament the gardens.

Students walk by, with their books, to the colleges.

Townspeople walk together to the village.

From parks and schoolyards, children's voices call.

Sunday mornings, churches ring their bells.

On a clear day, you can see the mountains

where children play, in winter, in the snow,

and long trails lead to streams and waterfalls.

Deer and mountain lions walk the mountains.

Rattlesnakes doze for hours in the sun.

Some days the ponds are visited by bears

who stumble home with their bellies full of trout.

Unable to sleep, I leave my house tonight

and sit at my wooden table under the trees.

Now the winds and birds have settled, the night is still.

The owl in the cedar tree begins to bell.

Rose and jasmine burn their sticks of incense.

Moonlight falls on Claremont through the clouds.

I remember Po Chui's poem about the cranes.

In the early dusk, down an alley of green moss,

the garden boy is leading the cranes home.

How strange and powerful, the love of home.

Stranger still, is to be alive at all,

to be anywhere, in all its endless detail,

and the millions of tiny locks that will be broken

before you can be released from where you are,

to return again forever to the place,

so many years ago, you started from,

the nothing that is everywhere but here.

Hotel

After a poem by Donald Justice, with the same title, the same form, and the same last line

One night, it seemed this grand and secret place
was their whole world, in which they felt at home,
walking down long halls to find their room.
Later, waiting for sleep, waiting for dawn,
it seemed the sounds of the city had been turned on,
horns and sirens blaring far away,
and planes droning past in the night sky
that they had almost forgotten was still there.
And then, at dawn, how strange to wake up here.

And not so grand or secret, after all,
they may have felt, walking through the lobby
and stopping in the little shop for coffee.
Beyond the plate-glass window was the world,
remembered now. Soon they would be hurled
into the daily storms and battles there.
And home seemed far away now, very far.
Perhaps she shed some tears, but silently,
and all was as it had been and would be.

A Brief Inferno

In the middle of my life, I had lost my way,
And found myself alone in a dark wood.
—Dante

Of course, we are always alone, always lost,
and always in the middle of our lives.
At least we hope there is enough time left
to finally get things right. If only, if only...

And the dark wood seems to be getting darker
as we try to find the path we wandered from.
The world looks strange and wild when you are lost.
Waiting somewhere out there is the witch.

You get up in the morning and you drive to work,
your eyes on the road, your hands gripping the wheel.

The Moon Of Creagan

There is nothing in books, only a few words.
−Robert Mezey

Walking out of my house early this morning,
I glanced up at the sky and saw the moon.
The world was full of light from a brilliant sun,
but the moon was a pale circle of gray and white,
as if it had been burning up all night
until, by morning, it was a small ash
left in the deep blue bowl of the cloudless sky.

Though I must have seen this moon before,
today I felt the thrill of recognition.
This is the moon of ash, the moon of Creagan.
I thought of Borges' poems about the moon,
his wish to say its true and secret name.
There are so many names, but with just one,
you can hang the moon in the sky over the poem,
shining in the radiance of its name.

Anyone who spends much time with words
will often wonder how they work their magic,
and understand the allure of the Kabballah.
These little strings of consonants and vowels
are all we need to dream the dreams of Shakespeare
and write the history of recorded time
and everything that we have learned so far

about the inexhaustible universe,
and everything we have so far left unsaid.
With the simple magic of the alphabet,
a poem can cast a spell down years of time,
as long as words are loved, as long as rhyme.

Years from now, in a quiet library,
paging through an old anthology,
someone may find these lines and see the moon
shining still in the sky over the poem.

I like to think the thrill will feel the same
as the thrill I felt today, in a distant time,
as, entering the story of the poem,
he will walk out of my house into the sun,
and glance up at the sky and see the moon,
and recognize the moon, and know its name.

Another Riddle

It would shatter us to know wholly our nature;
Out of his pity for us, God has given
Day after day, and then oblivion.

Borges, from *Oedipus And The Riddle*,
translated by Mezey and Barnes

They knew in the beginning what had started,
and this strange knowledge frightened the best of them.
They locked it up and tried not to remember.
For years, the memory still could make them tremble.
But this died out. And as the years came on,
by steady work, new rooms of thought to move in,
new pictures to be hung on all the walls,
were added to the house of intellect.

After how many years, we go on working,
knowing as we live from day to day
that night is coming, and oblivion.
And sometimes when the fragile lights are out,
we hear that scratching in the attic room.
It lives in the same house. How many midnights
have we paused on the stairs up to its door
and turned back, shaking, to our quiet beds?

Haiku

Words on the page like
stones on the streambed, your mind
flowing over them.

The quiet garden.
Falling asleep in sunlight,
before the hailstorm.

Sky of loud fire,
skyrockets, Roman candles.
And my dog, trembling.

Night. Loud orchestra
of frogs in the little pond,
suddenly quiet.

My African Grey,
Earl, looks formal, elegant,
singing *Duke Of Earl*.

The movie playing
tonight in the old folk's home
is *Forever Young*.

Bombay Sapphire, so
beautiful a name for this
clear fire-water.

Waking in our bed,
I reach for her, remember
she has gone away.

Saw my face today
in the mirror, recognized
someone I once knew.

Tumor in your lung.
What help now, the flea circus
of philosophy?

Reading over my
poems, always the same thought. So
much has been left out.

Even the atoms
are tired tonight, the quarks
turning off their charm.

What I am will soon
be gone, and then forgotten,
and my grave empty.

Night. The sound of rain.
Snow falling in the mountains
while I fall asleep.

Dark shapes are moving
over the mountains' green skin—
shadows of the clouds.

Moonlight falling through
clouds, and somewhere in the night,
the dreams of an ant.

The spring festival.
Villagers walk past graveyards,
silent temple bells.

My door left open.
I see a black cat walking
through my library.

Jacarandas

The jacarandas are in bloom again
and lavender blossoms are falling everywhere,
announcing the beginning of summer here,
in Claremont, California, this small town
of old houses, colleges and trees,
where I have lived for over thirty years.
In early June, the blossoms bloom and fall,
each lavender blossom like a little bell,
and their summer anniversary makes me smile.
Some hidden rhythm at the heart of things
summons them here each year to light and glory,
but the flowers bloom for only a little while,
and I am also in this rhythm's thrall,
and know, one summer, when the flowers come,
no one will find me here at this address.
A fading memory then, my name and face.
Some hidden rhythm at the heart of things
brings lavender blossoms snowing everywhere.
Days are passing, brief and beautiful.
The jacarandas are in bloom again.

A Good Day

The hot sun had gone down
at the end of a summer's day.
Good friends had gone home
and the children had gone to bed.
All the afternoon winds
had blown away somewhere,
and the world was clear and calm.
We were happy then
to let the evening come,
to sit outside at dusk
and watch the brush of darkness
touch the lawn and the trees,
and then the wall and the sky,
until it was finally night.
Some nights you would light a candle,
some nights we had the moon
and the sky was full of stars.
We would sit together and talk
until the words ran out,
and then we would come inside
and listen for the children,
safe and asleep in their beds.
We would make love then
and snuggle into sleep;
but before we fell asleep,

one of us would say,
Today was a good day,
and then the other would answer,
Yes. Yes it was.

Road Kill

Driving to the hospital late last night,
I turned down a road that ran between dark fields.
Up ahead, in the middle of the road,
a small brown rabbit was sitting very still,
looking down at a rabbit who was dead,
a mangled corpse, run over by a car.
Lit up by my headlights, he took off toward the fields.
Slowing down, I drove by the dead rabbit,
then stopped the car, and watched in the rear-view mirror.
The rabbit came back and sat in the road again,
resuming the vigil for his dead friend, or kin.
Quiet, still, he sat and stared at him.

Touched, unable to guess what you felt or thought,
I found it hard to watch you suffer this.
You have no words to understand what death is,
no words to ease your sadness, to console,
to mourn or pray, or tell your friend farewell.

I hope you made it safely home last night
and woke this morning in the warm sunlight.
This morning, at my table under the trees,
because you have no words, I've written these.

Jorge Luis Borges
1899-1986

for Bob Mezey, with many thanks for his wonderful translations of Borges

You have escaped the labyrinth of time,

escaped your poems, your stories and your name.

Your name, with its two dates, is carved in stone,

and printed here, on this page as white as stone,

but you have journeyed to oblivion.

No one will come here looking for your tomb,

and no one will find you there. Where you have gone,

no one can find you now but in a dream.

Dreams and mirrors always haunted you.

This poem will be a dream and mirror too.

In its flawed glass, let those who come here view

the images that consoled and tortured you.

Here is the moon, the tiger and the rose,

here the river of Heraclitus flows;

and each metonymic sword and dagger glows

with tales of the brave captains, toughs and gauchos.

Here is the labyrinth and library,

the books you loved and finally, could not see,

the histories of algebra and fire,

and music that reflects time in its mirror,
the atlases, theologies, and Shakespeare,
the chronicles of dynasties and war;
and Plato's ancient dreams about the pure,
Eternal Forms your father found so dear.

Here your last evening counting syllables
and shuffling rhymes until they chime like bells,
and the last time you sacrifice a pawn,
knowing the logic of the end-game soon
will force the now inevitable checkmate,
the mirror and the metaphor of fate.
The bar of sulfur glowing in a closet,
the treasured colors of your last sunset,

your father's face, kissed for the last time;
the mirrored face of Borges, growing dim,
but grave and calm, as you said farewell to him,
the last evening you waited for the dawn
so you could feel the blessing of the sun,
these memories now live only in a poem.
How many memories vanished with your ghost,
like flowers pressed in a well-loved book, and lost?

Alone, in a strange city, far from home,
awake all night, and waiting for the dawn,
but hoping for the calm of sleep to come,

why do I go on working on this poem?
Why do I suddenly feel I am no one,
that it is Borges, wherever he has gone,
into the secret night of oblivion,
who whispers these dear words that I write down?

After Reading A Review Of A Book Of Poems Which Is Praised For Being Free Of The Old Confines Of Rhyme, Free Of The More Rigid Forms Poetry Commanded In The Past

This book won a major prize, was highly praised.

Skeptical, but hoping to be surprised,

I bought the book, came home and read it through.

I should have known better. Here is *my* review:

Free from all the fetters of form and rhyme,

imagination, humor, wit and skill,

these are not poems at all, except in name.

Who'll read these poems with pleasure? No one will.

Some poets still are masters of the art.

If you want the real thing, here is where to start.

Read Justice, Mezey, Snodgrass, Wilbur, Hecht,

Borges, Larkin, Hall and Gunn, Coulette,

Frost and Stevens, Robinson and Hardy,

Miller Williams, Starbuck, Kennedy,

Barnes and Fairchild, J. V. Cunningham,

The Art Of The Lathe, The Exclusions Of A Rhyme.

Reading these books, I know what to expect,

familiar poems, with the power to touch me yet.

All the old masters I won't mention here,

just Martial and Catullus, Horace, Homer,

Po Chui and Chaucer, Donne and Wyatt, Shakespeare.

These are the poems I keep returning to

when I close an artless book, one more disaster.

And then I find what I am looking for:

artful free verse, poems in rhyme and measure,

instruction and delight, and the deep pleasure

of real poetry written by a master,

strong and clear and memorable and true.

The art is old. The poems are fresh and new.

Driving Down A Country Road
In The Rain

Today we drove in the rain down a country road.

The fields on either side were turning to mud

and cows were standing still in the cold rain.

My daughter saw the cows and said, *How cute!*

I told her I thought the cows might be depressed.

If the pastures were sprayed with Prozac, would the cows

run and frolic over the wet grass,

lifting their heads, licking at the rain?

We laughed, but I was reminded of the days

when I felt like a dusty field turning to mud,

or like a dumb beast standing in the rain.

Caveman

Last night I had a dream about a caveman
coming back from a long, unlucky hunt,
tired and thirsty, finding his long way home.
When he gets home, he learns his wife has been raped
and both her legs are broken. Some of his children
have been killed, and all the rest are dying,
and someone has shit in his cistern of rainwater.
With a rock, he helps his wife and children die,
then digs a hole with the rock and his bare hands,
so he can bury them. When he is finished,
he stands by himself and looks up at the stars
that have no names, not even the name *star*,
not knowing why, or what he's looking for.

Another Love Story

My girlfriend dumped me for a guy named Frank
and my heart did all the things a heart can do
when it is broken. Long nights, alone, I drank,
in my house that started smelling like a zoo,
wondering how my girl, whose love seemed true,
could leave me suddenly for someone new.

A few months later, I saw my former lover,
and could tell my hardest times were nearly over
as a great idea blossomed in my head.
Laughing, I walked up to her and said,
working my eyebrows in my best Groucho,
Hello sweetheart, can I be Frank with you?

Poem For My Dentist

This poem's for Dr. Gregrey F. Bodhaine.
Some poets might suspect that I'm insane
for using the austere art of formal verse
for one who drills, or pulls, my teeth, or worse.
I don't much care. You have been good to me.
You are a wizard of good dentistry.

Your skill and sense of humor make me smile.
I'm thankful for the magic you can do,
and hope this light verse brings a smile to you.
It's fun to play with words a little while,
forget the dreadful music of the drill,
the horror of decay, the root canal.

Before I met you, I would quake with fear
whenever I approached a dentist's chair.
But at your hands, I've suffered little pain.
You're a master in the art of Novacaine.

Over the years, my teeth have gone to hell,
in spite of cleanings, flossing, fluoride gel.
You've done your best to help my teeth get well,
a losing battle, started much too late.
Each morning I put in my upper plate,
and think of all the work still left to do.
I'm off tomorrow. I'll be calling you.

Telephone Greeting

You have reached 985-0732,
and so you have my number. This is true,
but I'm not here right now to talk with you.
I'm sure you know exactly what to do.

Please leave your number and your name, OK?
Then say whatever the hell you want to say.
The secret games that the electrons play
will save your words. Sometime later today,

when I get home, or struggle out of bed,
when I sober up, and finally clear my head,
my laundry's done, and all my books are read,
when all the cows come home, and God is dead,

my taxes paid, my accounts all in the black,
I'll check my messages, and call you back.

Fooling Around With
The Words In The Good Book

Many are called, but few are chosen.
Many are cold, but few are frozen.

And death shall come like a thief in the night.
Please come tonight, and take my wife.

Abandon all you have and follow me.
Homeless, lost, in utter penury,
will it help to contemplate the Trinity,
the Father and the Son, the Holy Ghost?
It little matters, since we'll soon be toast.

Blessed are the meek, for they shall inherit the earth.
So will the proud, the arrogant, the dull,
the heretic, the insanely criminal.
Let's not mince words. The earth inherits us.
All saints and sinners ride the same damned bus.

All of us one day will be underground.
On Judgement Day, if the angels' trumpets sound,
it will not matter, we will never hear,
nor rise in rapture. We will stay right here.

Father, Father, why have you forsaken me?
Nothing personal, Son, I do it randomly.

I am the Lord thy God. I can do whatever I want.

It's not in the Book, but it's my favorite taunt.

Lighten up, and laugh, as all my angels do.

I've made you in my image, as you know.

Your creator has a sense of humor too.

Rabbis and priests have been too hard on you.

Forget the Ten Commandments, and the Torah,

and book a two week cruise to Bora Bora.

Just remember to be kind to one another,

and kiss your kids today. And call your mother.

Snapshots From New Orleans

Last night, I photographed my teenage daughters
in a small, dark restaurant on Bourbon Street.
Sara and Rachel smiled at me. They were framed
by the wide window behind them, thrown open now
to the revelry and chaos on the street.
Their faces looked like masks of white enamel
in the eerie illumination of the flash.
I went on snapping their pictures in the dark.
Not innocent myself, nor sentimental,
I was surprised when it began to feel
like photographing angels lost in Hell.

Rain is falling now on New Orleans,
falling on its balconies and flowers,
on wrought-iron gates that open into gardens,
on drunks vomiting in the old, bricked alleys,
the addicts pushing needles in their veins,
on a teenage girl who cruises Bourbon Street
and lifts her blouse until she scores some beads.

Girls prowl the streets all night like feral cats.
Now one is cornered by a pack of men,
chanting, over and over, *Show us your tits!!*
She obliges them, and shows them more than that.
So many girls look younger than my daughters.
I imagine some are homeless, runaways.

Do fathers somewhere pray they're safe tonight?

My daughters still are innocent, I think,

as were these others once, not long ago.

A father is no protection for his children.

Here with my daughters, I am praying too.

For My Daughter, Sara,
On Her Nineteenth Birthday

I had flown back from Chicago late one night
and drove home from the airport into Claremont.
In the old, dark house on Kemper Avenue,
I found your mother in the library,
sitting under a lamp, reading a book.
We hugged and kissed. I sat down next to her
and started telling her about Chicago.
She listened quietly, and smiled at me.
I am pregnant with our daughter, Sara.
I was suddenly filled with so much happiness
but couldn't find the words to tell her this.
I walked across the room to the fireplace,
and watched the fire burn, and felt its heat,
and then came back and looked into her eyes.
And the great wheels smash and pound beneath our feet,
is what I finally said, smiling at her,
a line from Thomas Wolfe, and Donald Justice.
I have never been so happy, ever again,
unless perhaps on your and Rachel's birthdays.
My hands were the first hands to ever touch you.
I delivered you, then clamped and cut the cord,
then gave you to your mother. She held you, smiling,
and I was smiling, and Dick and Marilyn.
Perhaps you still remembered the dark ocean,

so calm, so lately crossed. Now you were loved,
in a world in which you felt that you belonged.

A few years later, you were sitting on my lap
watching a situation comedy
which showed a dead man in a funeral home.
You became quiet and you started to cry,
and then you said, *I don't want to die!*
I laughed. *Sara, you're only four years old,
with a long and happy life ahead of you.*
I know, you said, *but someday I will be old,
and I will be alone, I will be dying,
and then there will be no one who can help me.*
Your tears fell. You were inconsolable.
I held you tight, but found no words to say.
These are the words I want to say tonight.

Though I don't want to die, someday I will.
I want you and Rachel to be with me then.
We will help each other say our last farewell
and I will hold your hands and die in peace,
knowing I was blessed to be your father.
When you are dying, I will be with you.
You will remember me, and know I loved you,
and remember others who are dear to you.
You will feel tired, and then more tired still.

No longer frightening, or terrible,
death might seem a friend who'll come to fetch you
from a world where you no longer feel at home.
The day will come when you will feel it's best
to close your eyes at last, and finally rest.

I remember well one sunny afternoon,
when I sat on the grass under the Kafir plum tree
watching you and Rachel as you danced
on the patio outside the Kemper sun-room.
Marvin Gaye was on the radio,
singing *Sexual Healing*. You sang along
with Marvin Gaye, dancing with your sister,
and I watched and smiled, and wondered, and still do.

And I remember when you came to tell me
that you were going to run away from home.
Where will you sleep? I said. What will you eat?
We went into the kitchen, and ate our dinner,
and then you said it was time for you to go.
You packed some clean clothes in your little backpack,
and said good-bye, looking brave and sad.
I picked you up and held you in my arms.
I told you I wanted you to stay with us.
You started crying; I carried you up to bed,
and watched you then until you fell asleep.

A few years later, you were at Carden School.
I was the one who had run away from home,
living by myself, apart from you.
You sang a solo in a musical
and I was there to hear you sing your song.
How beautifully you sang, and stopped the show,
as everyone told me, after you were done.
Later that evening, when I went to bed,
I heard you singing as I fell asleep.

The years pass, but they are years, and full.
I can remember when you learned to talk,
how thrilled I was to hear you say my name.

Last year, I watched you graduate from high school
and now you're off to college, doing well.
Some weekends you drive home to visit us,
and Ricky, your sister Rachel, your boyfriend, Andrew.

Life is a short night in a bad hotel,
St. Theresa may have said. Life is, as well,
our only respite from oblivion,
our only chance to *know* and to be known.
Love called you here, and love gave you your name.
Thank you for coming here to be with us
to use the time that has been given you,
a gift more precious since it cannot last,

to work and love, to suffer joy and pain,
on the path you will walk down once, and never again.

You're beautiful, Sara, with eyes of the clearest blue,
eyes that can see into the tears of things,
and still light up with love and laughter too.
Dear, good daughter, I am proud of you.

My Parrots Talking To Each Other

Earl and Lola live in separate cages
in the same room. Earl is an African Grey,
formal, elegant, and very smart.
His feathers are gray, his tail-feathers are red.
Lola is an Amazon, colorful,
blue and green and yellow. She is bubbly,
very flirtatious, and she likes to sing.
Earl is laconic, with a good sense of humor,
and often speaks in my voice, which is low and dry.
One night I was reading in the living room
and heard my parrots talking to each other.
Hello Earl, Lola's here, say Hi
to Lola. Come on, Earl, say Hi to Lola.
Then Lola starts to sing, like a coloratura.
Earl interrupts her singing and says, *What?*
in my voice. Lola laughs, and tries again.
Hi Earl, Lola's here. Say Hi to Lola.
And then she sings. Earl listens for a while
and then he says, *Be quiet*! Lola laughs
and goes on singing. Earl listens again,
and then he raises his voice and yells, *Stop it!!*
Lola ends her song. Now she is quiet.
Earl laughs, and then he says to Lola, *Bummer.*

Prayer

When we are invited to a banquet, we take what is set before
us, and if we should ask his host to set fish on the table or sweet
things, he would be thought absurd. Yet we ask the gods for what
they do not give, though they have given us so many things.

Epictetus

Thank you for the universe, the world,
for earth and water, fire and fresh air,
for sunlight and the night sky full of stars,
the million-petalled flower of being here,
for music that reflects time in its mirror,
silence, darkness, rest and sleep, and dreams,
wind and rain, forgetting and forgiveness,
the love that holds together all there is.

I might have wanted something else, of course,
but tell me how I could have asked for this.

What I Am Afraid Of

I am afraid of the dark.
I am afraid of being abandoned
by persons who tell me they love me.
I am afraid of getting older,
though it has been going on
for a long time now, and nothing
terrible has happened.

I am frightened by ugliness.
I am frightened by the look of a child
who has suffered severe burns.
I am frightened of an image
of a woman in labor
whose knees have been strapped together.

Books

There are perhaps no days of childhood we lived as fully as those we spent with a favorite book. If we still happen today to leaf through those books of another time, it is for no other reason than that they are the only calendars we have kept of days that have vanished, and we hope to see reflected on their pages the dwellings and ponds which no longer exist.

−Proust

O the dwellings and ponds forever lost,
preserved only in memory and in books.
Books are the temporal lobes of civilization,
remembering all the words we've written down,
all the words we never want to forget,
along with a lot of noise and foolish nonsense.

The library burning in Alexandria–
a major stroke that damaged the mind of man,
so many thoughts and memories lost forever.

I remember the moment when I learned to read.
I was sitting at my desk in the first grade classroom
when the teacher wrote some letters on the blackboard:

B...R...O...W...N

I had learned the letters and their sounds
and suddenly I read the word BROWN.
I knew that something wonderful had happened.

Now I know my brain had changed forever.
Then I knew I could read anything
and everything, and of course I did.

My house is a library, full of well-loved books.
In my old age, I am learning to close softly
the books I know I will not be coming back to.

These books I will have with me when I am dying:
the poems of Donald Justice and Robert Mezey;
the poems of Borges, Horace and Catullus;
the poems of Philip Larkin and Po Chui;
and the words of Marcus Aurelius, Epictetus
and Seneca, and the essays of Montaigne.

When Death approaches and tries to frighten me,
I will remember the equanimity
Of Diogenes, when approached by Alexander.
Diogenes was sitting in the sun.
Alexander walked up to him and said,
I am Alexander, the great king.
I am Diogenes. I am the Dog-Man.
Is there anything I can do for you?
Please move a little. You are blocking the sun.

Perhaps I'll taunt Death with this quatrain by Coulette:

> *Where is it that the wise abide?*
> *What houses and what streets are theirs?*
> *Nowhere! Nowhere! The wise have died,*
> *In joy and silence, without heirs.*

Then Death will take me, unamused by my quiet laughter.

Memories From Childhood:
At My Grandparents' House

242 Alden Avenue
New Haven, Connecticut, my grandparents' house,
My father's parents, Paul and Mary Creagan

When I am dead, I'll be a long time dead,
my grandfather always said, late each night,
when my grandmother told him it was time for bed.

He would stay in his chair, and go on reading the paper,
and watch television, and talk to me.
I was only a boy, and he was an old man,
but we enjoyed each other's company.

Later, in bed, surrounded by the dark,
I would dare myself to overcome the dread
of saying the words my grandfather had said.

When I'm dead, I'll be a long time dead,
I would finally say out loud, but quietly,
then close my eyes and stare into the dark,
as if I was staring at eternity,
beyond my understanding. But I could feel it,
the way I could feel the immensity of the ocean
when I walked alone, at night, along the shore.

I remembered the lines from an old children's prayer,
and said the words, but found no comfort there.

I felt a sense of vertigo, and then
I was falling faster and faster into sleep,
hoping morning would come, and I would wake.

Memories From Childhood:
Four Years Old, Julie and I,
Behind A Pine Tree In Her Backyard,
Explore Each Other's Bodies

I still can smell the hay we sat upon,

behind the tree. We were quiet. We felt no shame.

We took off our clothes and then, when we were done,

we looked at each other, and strange new feelings came.

We had stumbled upon a mystery, and its spell.

For once, there was something new under the sun.

We shared a secret we could never tell.

We had no words to say what we had done.

First Death

My grandfather died when I was thirteen years old. I was raised in a strict Catholic family, and the God I had learned about seemed more concerned with justice and punishment than with mercy and love. After all, this God had created Hell.

My father drove me to the funeral home
the night before his father's funeral.
I walked across soft carpet to his side.
He was dressed in a black suit I had never seen.
He looked old and thin and pale, and very still.
He was a good man, what I knew of him,
but I had been good, and I had learned to sin.
I knew the jeopardy all souls were in.
Then something happened, something terrible.
I started crying. Hot tears began to fall.
Convulsive sobbing progressed to an anguished howl.
Alarmed, my father led me from the room,
and drove me home, and tried to comfort me,
not understanding why my tears still fell.
I tried to talk, but found no words at all,
and vowed in secret I would never tell
what made me feel so inconsolable.
I had seen a vision, and could see it still,
my grandfather screaming in the flames of Hell.

Ouija Board

For Ollie, who seems to understand these things

Jack and Lynda and I, one night in Pittsburgh.
We sat on the floor around the Ouija Board.
A candle was burning. We were watched by a black cat.

John was a friend of ours, now dead two years.
He had steered his car into a concrete abutment,
at seventy miles an hour, and killed himself.

Does John have anything to say to his friends?
Lynda asked, addressing the Ouija Board,
and soon the board answered, *Look at line 8.*

I smiled and thought, *This is ridiculous.*
Then a book fell from the shelf above my head
and landed in my lap, its pages open

to a French lesson I had written years ago,
when I was in college, when John was still alive.
On a lined page, torn from a spiral notebook,

I had written thirteen sentences in French.
On the next line, I had written the English translation.
We looked at line 8. I had written, years ago,

John est tres heureux de retrouver ses amis.
John is very happy to hear from his friends.

One Night

The first woman I loved was a black hooker
in a whorehouse, in a slum, in West Virginia.
Some friends from my Catholic college in Pennsylvania
drove me there one night for this rite of passage.
The girl was young and very beautiful
and I approached her as I would a saint.
Perhaps she was a saint, and so was I.
I told her she was beautiful, and then
words failed me, as I fear they will tonight.
This happened more than fifty years ago.
A green light bulb hung over the stained mattress
on which we played our parts in the old ritual
of one of life's great ancient mysteries,
breaking every law of God and man.

At The Book Signing

You don't know what love is.
—Charles Bukowski

Last night I drove to a local winery
and sat in a large room at a long table
with some other local authors, our books spread out
in front of us. My book was a book of poems,
titled: True Love Stories And Other Poems.
A heavy-set, middle-aged woman came up to me,
and picked up my book, and then she laughed out loud.
You don't know what love is, she said to me.
I wondered if she was a fan of Charles Bukowski.
No, really, she said, *tell me what you know.*
Not too goddamned much, to tell the truth,
but I wonder if perhaps you'd like to teach me,
is what I wanted to say, but I held my tongue,
and stood up and shook her hand and smiled at her.
She wasn't finished. *Do you have a wife?*
If you do, have you written a love poem just for her?
As a matter of fact, I have, I said to her.
I opened the book to a poem called **A Good Day**,
a poem I had written several years ago
when I was separated from my wife,
remembering a good day we once had shared.
She mouthed the words silently as she read,
then closed the book, and slammed it on the table.

God, it's beautiful, she said to me.

I'll buy your book, and make my husband read it.

She bought the book and then approached her husband,

who was pacing back and forth, waiting for her.

She opened the book, and held it out to him.

He turned away from her and left the room.

She closed the book, and sighed, and followed him.

No One Told Me It Would Be Like This

In spring, unruffled ponds reflect the light.
Fishermen bring home baskets full of trout.
Night has fallen and the stars are bright.
Let's go to bed, and blow the candles out.

Find me, she whispered, while we were making love.
I had no idea what she was thinking of,
but figured it out, and found myself as well,
and we trembled then, each like a struck bell.

All our words seem to turn from each other's arms.
Something is trying to live. I know its sweat,
how it tosses under its sheet in fever and dreams,
its chest sucking for all the air it can get.

We are losing each other, and we know it.
Why did we think our words would help with this?
Useless, our mouths will open and stay quiet,
tongues, numb with talking, touch and kiss.

Tonight I feel like a broken, old violin,
forgotten, lost, not played since God knows when.
The night is still, and still each dusty string,
and no one comes to touch them, help them sing.

No one told me it would be like this,
but I can remember small forebodings now,
the way that rainy Sundays made me feel,
and being punished, and waking up for school.

The iron fist inside the velvet glove.
The world is the fist, the glove its ornaments.

Walking In The Park With Sadie

Sadie and I were walking through the park.

A little boy came up to me and said,

"My name is Jacob, and I like your dog."

"Come here, Sadie, and say hello to Jacob."

His eyes got very big, and then he smiled.

"You mean," he said, "you have a dog who talks?"

"Not really," I said. He looked disappointed.

"Well, can she listen?" "Of course. Talk to her."

Quietly, Jacob said, "Sadie, come here."

Sadie came to Jacob. He stroked her fur.

He seemed to be waiting for her to talk to him.

I wanted to tell him that someday he would know

that *there is a world and we are alive in it*

is more amazing than a dog who talks.

Rebecca's Story

There once was a little puppy called Rebecca
who was born on an almond farm in Turlock, California.
A wonderful woman named Katy came to the farm
and sat on the lawn in front of the litter of puppies.
She watched them awhile, and then she said, *Come here.*
Rebecca was the one who came to her.
Katy brought her to me. She became Rebecca Creagan,
and I love her. Anyone would, of course.
And she loves me, more than anyone ever has,
or ever will. I am an old man.
From time to time, I tell Rebecca her story.
She listens to me, and looks at me with love.
I know she doesn't understand the words,
but she likes the sound of the words, the sound of her name,
and the sound of my voice when I tell her that I love her.

Euthanasia

For Molly, and for Janet, who told me this story

Molly was Janet's dog, a golden retriever.
They had many happy years together
as the very best of friends and loyal companions.
Molly knew when Janet was feeling blue
and she would stay close to her, to comfort her.
If Janet was crying, Molly would lick her tears
until Janet was calm, and her tears stopped falling.
Molly got old. She became diabetic
and needed shots of insulin every day.
Diabetes damaged her eyes, and she was blind.
Molly was suffering. Worse suffering would come.
Janet wanted to give her an easy death.

Molly lay on her side on a high steel table.
Janet stood next to her, and was holding her
when the vet began to inject the lethal drugs.
Molly didn't know what was happening,
but she knew that Janet was sad, Janet was crying,
and she began to lick dear Janet's face,
to lick away the tears that kept on falling,
as Molly was falling asleep, as she was dying.

Sad Night

The first phrase is a repeated phrase in the notebooks of Robert Frost

Dark, darker, darkest. This sad night
I am alone, and feel my only friends
are silence, darkness, Bombay gin, and smoke.

At Benjamin Pond

*Lines written before my friends brought me to
the hospital for treatment of alcoholism*

I sit on a bench beside the little pond
in the Botanical Gardens of Claremont. Surrounded by trees,
the pond reflects the trees and clouds and sky.
Turtles swim in the pond, and swarms of tadpoles,
blurring the mirrored world with quiet ripples.
Red-orange dragonflies are always here
flying back and forth across the water.
Now the turtles are basking on a rock,
and then the ducks float out upon the water,
dipping their bills for the bread I throw to them.

Approaching a fateful crossroad in my life,
I'm amused to contemplate the tadpoles here.
I know they also have no way of knowing
all the enormous changes soon to happen.
They will lose their tails, but then grow lungs and legs,
and leave the water for another world,
the world they dimly sense, perhaps, above them,
the world of earth and trees, and sky and air.

And what is going to happen to me? I wonder.
The sky darkens, and then comes rain, comes thunder.

For Doctor Harry

a good doctor, a good man, who has helped so many people at
Betty Ford, and who has helped me more than I could ever tell

Passionate doctor, passionate lecturer,
over and over again, you told us the truth,
because it is a matter of life and death.

Stay awake and pay attention. No sleeping here.
You have a fatal disease. There is no cure.
When you wake up the morning, say a prayer,
If you think you're doing well, have healthy fear.

Nothing is more important than your recovery,
not your job, your house, your girlfriend, or your money.
If anything else seems more important now,
then let it go. You'll lose it anyhow.
This disease is like a beast that's always there,
cunning, baffling, powerful, and more.
If you let your guard down, it will come out of its lair
to eat you alive. You're a doctor? It doesn't care.
It's an equal opportunity destroyer.
All the diplomas hanging on your wall
will not protect you now, and never will.
Remember how little help they were before.

When I wake up in the morning, it is there,
lurking in my closet, fouling the air
with its putrid breath. Believe me, I can hear
it breathing. And it knows that I am here.
It wants to destroy me, and I get sick with fear,
and get down on my knees, and say a prayer.

One day at a time, the old-timers like to say.
Keep working the steps. Work on one today.
Follow instructions. Get a sponsor. Pray.
Get yourself to meetings every day.
Don't allow yourself to wander from the pack.
Then you're easy prey and might not make it back.

Thank you Harry, for telling us the truth.
Alcohol, opiates, Ecstasy and meth
lead to the gates of insanity and death,
to police stations, hospitals and jails,
sad families getting dressed for funerals.
You introduced us to your brother, Dick,
also a doctor, who was killed by alcohol.
You keep his ashes in a little vial
attached to your key-ring. *May God keep his soul.*
You tell his story in order to warn us all
of what will happen to us if we're not careful,
if we can't be honest, and attend to the spiritual.

And you told us of your sponsor in Vermont,
the pizza maker, Anthony Tribuno,
three hundred and fifty pounds of good advice,
your Italian grandfather who had a nose for *boolsheet*.

Thank you for teaching us that we can heal,
and what we need to do to keep us well.
Thank you for helping us to hope and smile.
You are a higher power for us all.

Suicides Anonymous

Life has become unmanageable for us.
Welcome to Suicides Anonymous.

We meet each Friday night in the funeral home.
Will someone volunteer to read our poem?

Forget your 12 Step programs. They ask too much–
honesty, spirituality and such.

Our program's simple–one step and no relapse,
only eternal serenity, perhaps.

Has your Higher Power helped you out today?
What's a Higher Power anyway?

Our legal counsel will help you write your wills,
and we have knives and guns, and rope, and pills.

No abstention is required. Get drunk, get high!
Raise hell and have some fun before you die.

No one knows what's on the other side.
Death's a trip. Surrender, enjoy the ride.

You might like it, but you can't do it again,
and you'll have to give up dope and crack and gin.

Bill W's friends will be waiting at Heaven's Gate.
Eternal sober fun will be their fate.

May radiant angels serve you God's best wine.
Eternal aging makes the stuff divine,

and you can drink forever and a day–
there'll be no consequence, no hell to pay.

Keep coming back. It always works if you work it.
Come back to us as a wise and loving spirit,

and teach us how to take the step you took,
forget the coffee, the doughnuts, The Big Book,

and rise to Heaven's fellowship of friends,
high on serenity that never ends.

Transgressive Poem

Fuck all the bastards with an axe to grind.
This poem has something playful on its mind.

So do you want to fuck me in the ass?
Then all the critics grow erect, en masse,
and sound excited as they tell me this:

There is no poem, no author, only the text,
fixed in the historicity of its context,
determined by race and culture, politics,
and the gender of the genitals one licks.

I've heard this before from these pretentious pricks.

Long since I've crossed them from my reading list.
I'll write this poem to prove that I exist.

There was an old pervert with dentures
who liked to fuck Doberman pinschers.
Most dogs went along,
but one bit off his schlong.
Now he's looking for other adventures.

Poems are made of words, and words can sing,
can howl or scream, and sometimes they can hiss,
or whisper softly, softly, just like this.
Poems can sound like almost anything,

but if they sound as if they're smart and wise,
with special knowledge of what's real and true,
and how to separate the truth from lies,
tell them to go to hell, as I would do.

After Reading Wittgenstein

I write or try to write as if convinced that, prior to my attempt,
there existed a true text, a sort of Platonic script, which I had been
elected to transcribe or record.
       −Donald Justice

The object of philosophy is the logical clarification of thought

Language is self-contained. We can't step out of it.

Philosophy is a battle against the bewitchment of
our intelligence by means of language.

The right method of philosophy would be this:
To say nothing except what can be said.
       −Wittgenstein

The world is everything that is the case.
The mind's in the world. The world and mind embrace.

My language means the limit of my world.
Language is a net made out of words.
Thoughts, like butterflies, tremble in the net.
Babies and animals think without a language.
Dreams and memories, and wordless longings,
are naked thoughts until we find the words,
then wonder if our words are just and true.
That is not what I meant to say at all,
is what we often think of what we've said.

Donald Justice dreamed Platonic scripts
which he would try to translate into poems.
His poems are the dim shadows of the scripts.
There are closer and closer approximations.

Nothing you can sing that can't be sung,
the Beatles sang. But some things you can think
cannot be said, no matter how you try.
But there are closer and closer approximations.

Whatever can be said can be said clearly.
Whereof one cannot speak, one ought be silent.
This sounds like a statement of ethics, Wittgenstein.
Ethics are transcendental. So you said.
Perhaps you're alluding here to sucking cocks,
and not your ideas regarding thought and language.
It is known you suffered often from painful guilt.
Whereof one cannot speak, one ought be silent.

Some thoughts can't be caught alive in the language net.
In *Sunday Morning*, Wallace Stevens tells
of *things to be cherished like the thought of heaven.*
Passions of rain, or moods in falling snow;
Grievings in loneliness, or unsubdued
Elations when the forest blooms; gusty
Emotions on wet roads on autumn nights;

All pleasures and all pains, remembering
The bough of summer and the winter branch.
These are the measures destined for her soul.

There are more things in heaven and on earth
than are dreamed of in your drab philosophy.

*Not **how** the world is, is the mystical, but **that** it is.*
To this I bow my head and answer, *Yes.*

Why Is There Something

There are two ways of looking at the world. One way is to think there are no miracles. The other way is to think everything is a miracle.
    −Einstein

1. **Mysteries**

Long ago, on a morning no one remembers,
the first eyes opened in the universe,
and the universe could finally see itself.
This led to wonder, and endless questioning,
to poetry, physics, philosophy and prayer.
Why should there be something, rather than nothing?
Leibniz was able to dream the calculus
and ask a question that we cannot answer.
If you use his simple question as a mantra,
this meditation will leave you feeling dizzy
on the high wire over the abyss.
Newton also dreamed the calculus
and the numbers and the name of gravity.
Gravity is everywhere and nowhere,
and still its nature is a mystery,
though we know it holds the universe together
and keeps the planets orbiting the sun.
Newton thought of gravity as a force,
but couldn't explain its action at a distance
across the millions of miles of empty space.
Einstein imagined strange geometry

with gravity a distortion of space and time.

God does not play dice with the universe,

said Einstein, who was troubled by quantum mechanics,

the bubbling cauldron of probabilities,

the scary uncertainty at the heart of things.

Newton, locked in his house, studied alchemy

and looked in scripture for the names of God,

for prophecies and hidden revelations.

You are a soul dragging about a corpse,

said Epictetus. Is the ghost in the machine

the soul, the spirit, and a part of God?

How did mind arise from senseless matter?

How was senseless Matter blessed with Form?

Where did we come from? What did we come here *for*?

What secret are we trying to remember?

2. Animals

The lower animals differ from man solely in his almost infinitely larger power of associating together the most diversified sounds and ideas.
—Darwin

Language is confronted by a truly boundless terrain, the essence of all that can be thought. It must therefore make infinite employment of finite means, and is able to do so by the power which produces identity of language and thought.
—Humboldt

The secret we are trying to remember
is that we are animals, gifted animals,
blessed and cursed with minds that know so much,
and blessed with language, which changes everything.
Do we have souls? We have the gift of life,
a concept more intriguing than the soul,
and more amenable to investigation.
Go to the zoo and look at the animals:
the giraffe, the lion, the tiger, and the zebra,
the elephant, the camel, the kangaroo.
Then come home and play with the little dog who loves you.
Each animal is the glorious result
of one of the forking paths of evolution.
And so are we. All of our fellow creatures
seem to be innocent of thoughts of death,
but we know, for certain, that someday we will die,
and the world we tried so hard to understand,
the world, our only home, will be lost forever.

The Mind And The Brain

The Mind And The Brain, a book by Jeffrey M. Schwartz, M.D., presents compelling evidence from neuroscience which shows how the mind, by a power of mental force, can alter the functioning, and the physical structure, of the brain.

The mind is what the brain does.
—Steven Pinker

The brain starts the mind. What a strange entanglement,
when the mind is the maestro, the brain its instrument.

Materialist thinks that everything is matter.
He has a mind, but thinks it doesn't matter.

Dualist would like a ghost in the machine
for which no trace of evidence can be seen.

The world is everything that is the case.
The mind's in the world. The world and mind embrace.

To thrive in the world is the mind's accomplishment.
The brain is necessary, but not sufficient.

Our brains are similar; our minds are not.
The brain knows nothing. The mind is thrilled with thought.

The mind mints coins to put in the brain's purse.
Did my mind or my brain dream up this little verse?

To Thank John Bernoulli,
For A Memorable Line

John Bernoulli, a professor of mathematics,

in Basel, was also a Doctor of Medicine,

a philosopher. In 1696,

he published a difficult mathematical challenge:

to determine the equation of a curve

down which a bead would slide, from one point to another,

not directly beneath it, in the shortest time.

Mathematicians submitted their solutions,

among them Leibniz, L'Hopital and Newton,

The latter's solution was anonymous,

sent without his famous signature.

Bernoulli studied it and quickly saw

it was the work of Newton. How could he tell?

I recognize the Lion by his claw.

Old Words

Up in the crowded attic of the mind,
all the old words are stored. And you can find
them packed in boxes, or in the creaking drawers
of dusty, antique, mahogany armoires.

Vocatur Atque Non Vocatur Deus Aderit

Called or not called, the god will come.

Carl Jung inscribed this ancient Latin proverb over the door of his house

Hermes was the messenger of the gods.
Who'll bring the good news now, when Hermes nods?

Perhaps our eyes won't see, our ears won't hear,
even if the god might come so near.

You see what you're looking for, and recognize.
God came to Moses and Abraham, who were wise,

and spoke to them. What if the god should come
to prophets who are blind and deaf and dumb?

Then there would be no words to tell of him,
no scripture, no commandments, prayer or hymn,

only a feeling of loss when the god had gone,
as the blind can feel a cloud obscure the sun.

Auto Da Fe

The heresiologist is feeling glum.

He's having doubts, the seeds of heresy.

Long years he's done his awful work for God,

finding heretics and burning them,

if torture couldn't move them to confess.

He can't forget the smell of burning flesh,

the howls and screams provoked by his instruments:

the rack and wheel, the strappado, the iron maiden,

the red-hot pincers and the molten lead.

Burning heretics was an act of faith,

but now he recalls with terror the words of Christ:

Let him who is without sin cast the first stone.

What you do to the least of my brethren, you do to me.

God have mercy on my soul, he prays,

knowing God will soon be judging him.

He dreams of living in a far-off village,

and teaching the little children in the school

the boundless mercy of a loving God.

The World According To The Weekly World News

The last line is from a poem by James Crenner

Dragons stampede through Chinese villages.

Hitler is alive in Argentina

writing a comic novel based on his life.

The bones of Jesus have been found in Jerusalem,

and the bones of Adam and Eve in the Garden of Eden.

The Loch Ness Monster died giving birth to twins.

The Abominable Snowman will skate in the Ice Capades.

An asteroid will collide with our blue planet,

and scientists worry the sun might soon burn out.

The Face on Mars is beaming messages

from an advanced, extinct civilization

that came to earth in spaceships long ago

and helped the Egyptians build the pyramids.

A man who claims to have escaped from Hell

says he misses his friends, and will be going back.

A reptilian will be elected president.

The cure for cancer was discovered years ago,

but has been kept a secret from the public

thanks to drug companies and evil doctors.

This universe is an early poem of God.

According to our sources, His revision

will finally resolve the thorny problem of evil,

a stumbling block for even His staunchest fans.

The secret of life can be found on page eleven:
Be always amazed and amused, and always exult
in the life-long thrill of knowing you will die.

Personal Ad

I'm a single white female, pushing eighty,
with terminal lung cancer spreading in my brain.
But I am young at heart. My name is Katy.
I'll tell you what I want, and say it plain.

I want someone who will love me, love me well,
a special someone whose love I can return.
My body is ruined; it has gone to hell,
but I am full of love and lust. I burn.

There must be someone out there in this fix,
someone longing for a brief romance,
for a lover who might teach you some new tricks,
and share your sad last days, and your last dance.

So call me if you want to arrange a date.
Time is of the essence. Please don't wait.

On First Looking Into Internet Web Sites Which Had Recently Posted Paparazzi Photos Of Celebrities Behaving Badly

Then felt I like some watcher of the skies
When a new planet swims into his ken;
Or like stout Cortez when with eagle eyes
He stared at the Pacific—and all his men
Looked at each other with a wild surmise—
Silent, upon a peak, in Darien.
—Keats

Think far ahead with me, stifle the jeers,

and sympathize with some young kid in tears,

stoned on weed and far too many beers,

who finds one day, confirming his worst fears,

what's been displayed on the Internet for years,

the genitals of his mother, Britney Spears.

Limericks, And Other Trifles

My Patient In Room One Today

There was an old pervert from Serbia

who whipped out his dick, in suburbia.

Some kid called the cops,

and they collared old Pops.

Now his dick will no longer disturb ya.

A Silly And Affectionate Limerick For My Dog

My beautiful canine companiel,

Rebecca, a Brittany spaniel,

truly loves to hunt birds,

as I love to hunt words–

this poem's for The Bird Hunters Manual.

Cautionary Tale

If you're dreaming of pie in the sky,

you've succumbed to a damnable lie.

You married a witch,

your life is a bitch,

and some day you'll keel over and die.

For Someone Who Mistakenly Described Me As A Sensitive Poet, And A Gentle Physician, Who Drives A Muscle Car To Sublimate The Few Sparks Of Aggression I Am Able To Muster

A sensitive poet I'm not,

nor a gentle physician. *Mein Gott*!

I am kind but aggressive,

all my poems are transgressive,

and my Mustang is slicker than snot.

You Can Leave Your Hat On

There is a young lady called Yuly

who is secretly loved by yours truly,

who'd look hot in a hat

and in nothing but that,

except for high heels and some jewelry.

Ecological Couplet

The cost of milk and beef becomes quite dear

when the farts of cattle pollute the atmosphere.

On Growing Up With A Younger Brother, Who I Loved Dearly, But Who I Knew Was Much Smarter Than I Would Ever Be

I had to learn your brain was a red Ferrari

and mine an old, and rusted, orange Volkswagen.

Still, it took me where I wanted to go.

Back In The Sixties

Back in the sixties, I confess that, for better or worse,
I experimented with drugs. It was a crash course,
but I learned so much I gave myself a degree:
Michael Creagan, M.D., L.S.D.

Now at the end of a long and busy day,
after pouring a warmed snifter of Grand Marnier
and lighting a Camel, I proceed to make things worse,
and publish my bad habits in light verse.

Mulling Over An Old Chinese Proverb

The mind is a good servant, but a terrible master.
But who is the mind the slave or master *of*?

After Experience

Think you if Laura had been Petrarch's wife,
He would have written sonnets all his life?
—Byron

Marriage should be against the law, she said,
after she married me. Agreed as read.

Samuel Johnson, Describing Meaningless Activity

Sir, this is like getting on a horseback on a ship.
So is being born. And all the rest of your life.

The Proud Grandfather, A Fireman, Addresses His Little Grandson

What do you want to be when you grow up?

I want to be a gynecologist.

Little Verses

Kafka

How to go on, into oblivion,

not knowing why you were born, or who you are?

I think of Kafka, waking to blood on his pillow,

the daily horror of the sputum jar.

Lines Written In A Bad Mood, To The Muse

I wanted to leave you. I missed my chance.

Now you have me by the balls.

For you, each night, I go out and dance,

on the tightrope, over the falls.

Publishing

No longer hooked on their lines,

still I print my poems,

showing my helpless love

for the cages I've broken out of,

the coops I've built and flown.

Christmas Eve, Wrapping The Children's Presents

I want to give you something like peace, or like joy,

things that no one can give to anyone,

but I wrap up all of your toys that will break, or get lost,

and wonder who it is that is hurt the most.

Poem Smoking A Cigarette
In A Dark Corner Of The Page

I am not about to answer your question
in this poem. There is a certain amount
of mystery in any good relationship
which is not to be confused with misunderstanding.

Or would you like to see the Abominable Snowman
on the Johnny Carson show, talking about
his cameo appearance in the Ice Capades?

A Shell

A shell washed by water into sun
recalls the water, whispering its sound.
But you, my skull, my bone, how will you keep
the memory of this dream when I am gone?

Platonic Monologue

Tell your one, should she presume to complain
about your many, that they are false. Explain
that knowing them brings knowledge, though unsure,
which in the end will lead you back to her.

Dry Lament

And though I know I'll never find the reason
that, without reason, I have from Heaven
this curse I struggle under, being human,
I know, for what it's worth, the curse is common.

Why There Is A Monument Named After Him

We know he cut down cherries as a boy,
although the books all say he'd never lie.

He fathered the country, made that his career.
Word has it he slept almost everywhere.

How hard it must have been to get that done.
Erect a phallus, then, for Washington.

Mulling Over Philosophy, And Katy

What is the Good, the Beautiful, the True?
This is the hard work philosophers love to do.
To say *what* they are, I'll leave to this prolix crew,
but I know *where* they are, when I'm with you.

Learning To Talk

You will soon learn to talk.
I would like to hear you say
my name. But I am sorry,
for there is an old curse.

You will have thousands of words
and you will know what you know
and there will be whole years
when you say nothing at all.

The Silence Of Books

The silence of books is like

the sound of the tree falling

deep in the empty forest.

Will the book ever tell its story?

Will anything ever happen?

Now you open the book

and begin to read. Now

you can hear the tree falling

deep in the empty forest,

now the words on the page

flare up, like coals when the wind comes.

Limericks For Nuns

Be a nun. Get none.

*Albolene is the brand name for a make-up remover which
leads a quasi-secret life as a prized sexual lubricant*

A sweet girl named Jill from Nantucket
sometimes walked down the hill with her bucket,
not to fetch some fresh water,
nor to do what you thought, Sir,
but to find her guitar, and to pluck it.

The nuns of The Holy Conception
were the young priest's unholy obsession.
He'd say: *Take off your habits,*
and let's screw like rabbits.
In the morning, I'll hear your confession.

A beautiful sister named Jean
found the rules of the convent obscene–
Lights out at seven,
Candles out at eleven–
but thanked God for her dear Albolene.

An Old Monsignor from New Jersey Addresses His Lover, Mother Superior

I know you've been craving affection.

During Lent, I can't have an erection,

but I'll take some Levitra,

and we'll celebrate, Easter,

the good Lord's, and my dick's, resurrection.

In Praise Of Chastity

A sonnet for Ian, who sparked my imagina-
tion with his thoughts on *the price of love*

my apologies to Shakespeare for mutilating his line:
The expense of spirit in a waste of shame.

Many the nights I spent with saucy whores
until I woke up with a tell-tale rash,
a chancre on my dick, and running sores.
I was bankrupt spiritually, and out of cash.

Thank God for Penicillin. I took the cure.
No longer would spirochetes party in my brain,
and I resolved then to be chaste and pure
and rid my life of penury and pain.

As always, William Shakespeare said it best.
The expense of semen in a wasted dame
will only bring brief pleasure, then unrest,
and long and sleepless nights of guilt and shame.

What is the price of love and fragrant gash?
Lend yourself a hand, and bank the cash.

Surprise

Jokes and magic tricks and poetry
all traffic in the pleasure of surprise.
Surprise and her timid sister, Novelty,
jolts the dull brain's neurochemistry
and good news flashes through its hemispheres.
Imagine all the neural fireworks
when Houdini made the elephant disappear.
Words play in the theater of the mind
with its smoke and mirrors, trapdoors, threads and wires.
Women magicians show off their cunning stunts.
In the magic cabinet of metaphor,
Juliet turns into the sun, and then the sun
pulls the world each morning out of night's black hat.
In Rilke's *The Archaic Torso Of Apollo*,
the poet feels the statue commanding him:
You must change your life. Moishe had read Rilke
as a young man, and took these words to heart.
When he was old, talking with his friends,
they asked him why he seemed to be depressed.
I worked hard for years to earn my reputation.
I was Moishe, the master-builder, the master-carpenter.
Once I was loved and respected in this town.
He looked sad and bewildered. *But you fuck one pig.*

Sentence

A sentence diagrammed with empty chairs.
The parts of speech will come and take their places.

What does the sentence say? Not very much.
If you have something to say, go ahead and say it.

Words For Tombstones

1.

Carved in stone, these words were once my own.
Now you can read them and remember me,
though I'm no longer what I used to be.
Slow time has turned me into skull and bone.

2.

I don't remember dying, but I did.
My bones lie here beneath the coffin's lid.
Who reads these words, consider what they say:
You will join me underground someday.

3.

Mother of the Muses, goddess of Memory,
please come with me, divine Mnemosyne,
when I set out to wander as a ghost,
and help me to remember what is lost.

4.

Now long out of my way are death and taxes.

Sad Poems

I like your poems, but it's a shame the way your life is.

from a fan letter

a grim chronicle of death, divorce and loneliness…

from a review of my first book, in the Philadelphia Inquirer

1. As the current saying goes, *It is what it is.*
I've distanced myself from the sturm and drang of po biz

and learned to accept the blessing and the curse
of turning my existence into verse

while my life has often veered dangerously off course–
into alcoholism, bankruptcy, divorce,

unscheduled vacations in pricey loony–bins,
and flirting with the seven deadly sins.

2. When I show my poems to my friends, they often tell me,
*You must have been really depressed when you wrote these
poems.*

This irritates me. I am sometimes depressed,
but never when I write. Almost never.

Who cares? The poems have a life of their own.
The artist is off to the side, paring his fingernails,

or putting a gun to his head, but it doesn't matter.
Of course, outside the poem, everything matters.

I love my friends. I worry about them too.
Sometimes I wonder if they are ever sad.

Gently, I ask them, *Are you happy with your life?*
They pour out their troubles. Then they begin to cry.

Then I console them with sad and bitter poems.

Truth And Beauty

Things change. Alternatives exclude.

A definition of evil by John Gardner

What are Truth and Beauty doing tonight?
I haven't heard about them in quite a while.
Perhaps they are living in a trailer park
somewhere in Pomona, California,
under assumed names, like Paul and Belle.
At night they walk outside and look at the stars
and remember the Heaven they descended from,
the Platonic realm where everything is perfect.
Now they live in the world of imperfection
whose history is like a Tarantino movie–
unspeakable evil, delirious revenge.
Here things change, alternatives exclude.
Love affairs end in jealously or boredom.
But there are moments of astonishment.

Now only mathematicians and physicists
remember them, and claim they are embodied
in their elegant theories and equations.
They are bewildered by modern poetry.
Pointless, frigid, fancy bullshit! says Truth.
The rhythm and melody are missing, says Beauty.

None of the poets ever mention them
unless to suggest they are ridiculous concepts
of an archaic and unenlightened age.
No absolutes! All truth is relative
and beauty is in the eyes of the beholder.
Favorite poems they keep in a wooden box
and read them often when they're feeling blue.
They tease each other after reading Keats.
I'm not you, and you're not me, says Truth.
Still, I like the way it sounds, says Beauty,
though I haven't the faintest idea what it means.

Soon they will go back to the World of Forms,
the museum of perfect things, the perfect pencil,
the perfect dildo, the perfect fork and spoon.
After their experience in this world,
they know perfection will take some getting used to,
and they might even miss the stone in the shoe,
the ants on the watermelon, the tarantula
on the wedding cake, the rainy Sundays, even
the dog shit on the antique Chinese rug.
They will miss the moments of astonishment.
Perfection can be boring. After all,
how many hours can you be amused
watching the ideal dog chase the ideal cat?

Every night before they fall asleep,

in their separate beds, there's something they like to do.

Together they read the poems of Donald Justice.

When they close the book, one of them always says,

The poems aren't perfect, but they're beautiful and true.

Little Song

Save the eagles,
love the beagles,
land a spaceship on the moon.

Do your Kegels,
eat your bagels,
maybe you'll be happy soon.

Atheist Holidays

Atheist Monica
celebrates Hannukah,
celebrates Easter and Christmas day too.

Laughing at reverence,
she opens her presents,
enjoying the ritualized hullabaloo.

After Reading An E-Mail From My Brother Telling Me That An Old Girlfriend Had Died at 71 Of Heart Failure

We fell in love when we were seventeen.
We danced each slow dance every Friday night
at Paradise Park, our bodies pressed together,
her pussy rubbing on my trembling thigh.

The last time I saw her was fifty years ago,
but so many memories are fresh in my mind's eye,
in which she always will be seventeen,
always young and always beautiful.

She starred in all my favorite fantasies,
but now she's dead, I'll sadly let her go.
Dead girls are out of bounds for me, although
they seemed to turn on Edgar Allan Poe.

Diatribe In Dactyls, and Other Verses

Meter is fascist, elitist as well,
and this bullshit some poets are eager to sell.
But our fondness for rhythm is primal and primitive,
something we're born with, not learned in a schoolroom,
and counting is something all children can do.

Chaucer and Shakespeare and Milton and Wordsworth,
and Wyatt and Rochester, Thomas Carew,
and the Brownings and Robinson, Stevens and Frost,
and George Starbuck and Kennedy, Justice and Mezey,
and Wilbur and Cunningham, Anthony Hecht,
Thomas Hardy and Larkin, to name just a few,
and the nursery rhymes written by Mother Goose too,
and the authors of song lyrics, what rappers do–
all of them writers of metrical verse,
and were all of them fascist, elitist, or worse?

Who the hell could believe this? Who thinks it is true?
Only irrational, hyperpolitical,
assholes and idiots mindlessly do,
and these dactylic verses are fucking with you.

On A Strange Poem by Yeats

A Stick Of Incense
Whence did all that fury come?
From empty tomb or Virgin womb?
Saint Joseph thought the world would melt
But liked the way his finger smelt.

Saint Joseph finger-fucks the Virgin Mary.
Mother of God!! Was this poem necessary?
Even great poets sometimes swing and miss.
He won the Nobel Prize, but not for this.

Baseball Fan, On Poetry
Talking about a famous, fancy poet:
He's technically perfect, but he never cuts to the bone.
He might have a fastball, but he doesn't throw it,
only change-ups, curves and sliders cross the strike zone.

Haiku

A golf ball shining
in the grass, like a tiny,
cratered, fallen moon.

A dandelion
on the lawn, a little cloud
tethered to its stem.

I am meeting you
on this quiet bridge tonight.
The bridge is language.

Existentialism

Do aficionados of existential dread
look forward to the peace of being dead?

Martin Heidegger

German philosopher, strange Martin Heidegger,
authored a book he called Being and Time,
writing, as someone besotted with Being,
a tortuous, dense philosophical gem.
Dying, he must have been hurt by the knowledge
that Being was not so besotted with him.

Thoughts On My Birthday,
Turning Seventy

It has been proposed that our entire universe was a vacuum fluctuation,
not caused but simply one of those things that happen from time to time.

From the Mystery of Existence, edited by Leslie and Kuhn

The fact that we human beings–who are ourselves mere
collections of fundamental particles of nature–
Have been able to come this close to an understanding of the
laws governing us and our universe is a great triumph.

From The Grand Design, by Stephen Hawking and Leonard Mlodinow

Some of the ancient thinkers like to say:
Truly it is the best of fates never
to be born. If I'd had the chance,
this is what I would have said to them:
Come fucking on, you miserable stupid pricks,
this is the only fucking game in town,
the only fucking game in the universe.
You've won the ontological lottery.
Against incredible odds, you are here,
here with your mind and body and your name.
You have a mind that knows and can be known,
and you have Time in which all Being dwells,
and you can say like God, I Am Who Am,
at least for a little while before you die.

The scientists of humor have concluded
that ducks are the funniest animals in jokes.
A woman with a duck on a leash enters a bar.
The bartender says, "Where'd you get the pig?"
The woman says, "You asshole, can't you see it's a duck?"
The bartender says, "I was talking to the duck."

Why should there be something, rather than nothing?
Gottfried Leibniz considered this simple question
the fundamental problem of metaphysics.
There is something funny about this,
a human being asking a simple question
that he knows only God could ever answer,
in a language he might never understand.
Imagine a duck trying to understand
the fundamental theorem of calculus.

Imagine a physicist trying to understand
the fundamental problem of metaphysics.
Physicists are joining the conversation,
but all they have to say is worthless bullshit.
Clearly, they don't understand the question
and they don't understand what nothing is.

And reductive materialism will never explain
what it's like to be a human being,
a little god who shits and laughs and loves.

The eventual heat-death of the universe
will snuff out any chance of being born,
at least in the only universe we know,
and will edit out our lives and all our words
as if they were typos in the sacred text.
All the libraries will be cold and dark
and no one will come to turn the pages there.

Here's a question closer to the bone:
Why should I be someone, rather than no one?
We find our own good answers every day
as we put off our plans for suicide.
The doors to oblivion are always open,
but we won't be invited back again.

We live like gods, and then we die forever.
This is our glory, this our bitter fate.

An Autumn Afternoon

Another autumn afternoon in Claremont,
my little town of colleges and trees.
I am an old man in a quiet house,
thinking on things beyond my understanding.
I look around the room and see my books
on wooden bookshelves lined along the walls,
and on my library table made of oak.
What did I learn from reading all these books?
Perhaps only the exquisite pleasure
of reading finely crafted sentences
that embody a clear and memorable thought.
I am sitting in my old blue leather chair.
Rebecca, my faithful dog, sits next to me.
I reach over and caress her noble head.
This and that, and everything I see,
and cannot see, everything there is,
is contingent on the ancient mystery
of why there should be anything at all,
rather than nothing at all. But here I am,
alive in the world of Being, the tiny island
in the vast ocean of Oblivion.
Answering a question with a question,
God once said to Job: *Where were you*
when I laid the foundations of the world?
If there is a God, I'd like to hear some answers,

but hearing from God would be a miracle
and I do not believe in miracles.
And then suddenly comes a surprising thought:
That I am here in the world is a miracle.

Fantasy For The Medical Profession Whose Members Are Bravely Clinical Even When Tested By Overwhelming Loveliness

The doctor is examining the new patient.

The nurse is standing by as a chaperone.

The nurse is pro forma because the patient

is a beautiful young lady and one never knows.

When the doctor is finished, he tells the young lady

her face is so beautiful it frightens him,

her skin is so lovely he can hardly bear to touch it,

her breasts are unforgivable,

and the rest of her body leaves him utterly speechless.

The patient is feeling better.

She is beginning to smile.

The doctor is taking off his clothes which is only fair

since she has already taken off hers.

She throws the hospital gown out the window

and it floats down like a deflated angel.

The schizophrenic patient in the next bed

has seen enough. She throws herself out the window,

sane for the rest of her life.

She splashes into a lake and swims away.

All the other patients in the hospital

are about to be healed by what is about to happen.

Even the lame will walk to the nurse's station tomorrow

demanding to be discharged against medical advice.

At last the lovers are in bed together.
They tell the flabbergasted nurse
that all of her patients have their lights turned on
and need her right now. She turns away quickly
and gives an injection to the wall
before she makes it out of the room and the door closes...

When the nurse gets home to her husband later that night,
they make love for the first time in twenty years.
The young lady, who is not really ill after all,
sings the chorus from Mahler's Eighth
all the way home on the bus.
And the doctor too is feeling much better
who previously had been feeling mildly depressed
and altogether too formal.

For My Children

Written when my children were living apart from me after a divorce

Before I would go to sleep,
I would come into your room
and look at both of you sleeping.

I would remember a line
from a poem: a father is no
protection for his children.

I thought of a good magician—
his wife turns into his lover
and his children are happy.

I would wish you good dreams
and then kiss you good night.
I was always amazed to see

how furiously your eyes
were jerking back and forth
under your closed eyelids.

One night I imagined a star
that can see everything,
a star that understands

and wants to make something happen,
but cannot, and understands,
and stays in the sky, and burns.

I would have said a prayer
if I had known how to pray.
It felt like I was praying.

Sean and Michael, I love you,
I have always loved you,
I will always love you.

I will stay in the sky and burn.

Nam Myoho Renge Kyo

Life is a struggle, you said,
but you wanted to give me some words
that can help anything happen.

I needed your help, you said.
Everything is connected;
there are no accidents,

and why else in the world would I call you
in the middle of the night
from somewhere in San Francisco?

Far out! Well, Hi!
What's gone on in your life
for the last ten years?

When I woke up this morning
I was thinking of you.
All day it seemed important

to try and tell you this,
and that was why I called,
or why I said I called.

But maybe you were right.
I know I needed your help.
And maybe you needed someone

to prove to you once again
that everything is connected;
there are no accidents.

And maybe you called me,
or something was calling us
to be together at midnight.

I don't know what happened,
or what was being connected
more than my voice and yours,

and after ten years,
from San Francisco, from Boston.
I don't know what happened,

but Christ, it was scary
after the ringing stopped
until I could hear your voice:

Is this Betsy? Yes.

Putting Her To Bed

Getting into bed, she sees a spider,

black and furry, climbing down the wall.

Scared, she runs to me a short time later,

asking if I'll stay with her a while,

to see if it comes back. So she'll feel safer,

I read her a story, get her a drink of water,

cover her up, let her turn off the light,

then leave her there, lacking anything better,

where she'll hide under the blankets, huddled tight,

and wait for the spider to crawl over her.

Alba

After the line: *Ah God, ah God, the dawn, it comes how soon*

French, 12th century

Not long ago,
when last the sun
put down his head,
leaving us to bed
to get undone,
let warm blood flow
and headway make, as lovers know,
I thought of dawn,
how it would come
before I'd come and gone
enough, and then some,
how the cock, bright red,
would scream, and said:
Ah God, ah God, the dawn, it comes how soon.

Helplessly,
we rode all night.
Were you a horse,
(begging your pardon, of course)
and I a knight,
I swear that we,
from France, could have made Italy.

I thought of dawn,

wished it would come

before my flesh was gone,

or torn, or numb.

Frantic, half-dead,

still dying, I said:

Ah God, ah God, the dawn, it comes how soon.

At last it came.

At last I rose

and got away.

I thought of you all day,

pulling on clothes,

calling my name.

Lady, you'll never be the same.

Neither will I,

glad to tell.

I think that bye and bye,

tonight as well,

I will return,

again to learn:

Ah God, ah God, the dawn, it comes how soon.

After Reading The Closing Of The American Mind On A Visit To Hawaii

Tonight the tourists chatter at the luau,

drowning out the muted cries of the peacocks.

A man from Ohio, who says he is "in computers"

is telling dirty jokes to a couple from Kansas.

I walk around, listening to conversations,

and get the impression that most of the people here

hate their husbands, their wives, their jobs, even their children.

I have no idea what they love.

How wonderful it is to contemplate the banality of evil

in a setting of such natural beauty, and to sit on the beach,

as I did this afternoon, reading an angry book

that attacks the university system in America

for failing to provide a truly classical education.

Even in a democracy, hell is other people,

no matter what they might have learned in school.

I have always considered myself a good Stoic,

but now I feel I am becoming a Cynic.

I remember the story about Diogenes

walking through the town with his lamp at night,

telling whoever asked what he was doing

that he was looking for one honest man.
I wonder if I have been an honest man.
He could sometimes be an insufferable prick,
although he also had a sense of humor.

One night he was hanging out in a dark tavern
with some philosophers. They were debating
the paradox of Zeno that was said
to prove the impossibility of motion.

Diogenes listened to the conversation,
and after a while, when he had heard enough,
he stood up and walked around the room,
proving the possibility of motion.

Back at the luau, the idiot from Ohio
is telling another joke, and the wife from Kansas
spills her colorful drink on her husband's shirt.
The tourists are louder. Looking for peace and quiet,

I walk down the winding path to the beach,
and let the warm trade winds, blowing off the Pacific,
soothe my fevered brain, and my bad sunburn.
I think of Demosthenes standing on a beach

with pebbles in his mouth, making himself
speak loudly and clearly over the sound of the waves.
What did he have to say that was so important?
Someone walking by lights a cigar

and smoke floats up like the soul leaving the body.
The stars are shining like the eyes of the ancients.
The tourists now are walking on the beach.
Everybody decides to go for a swim.

Later that night, when everyone is asleep,
there is an earthquake in Los Angeles
and small waves start out on their long journey.
Socrates drinks his hemlock, and asks for more.

For The Patients In Western Psychiatric Hospital

I think of you tonight
as I sit here quietly
marking these white walls.

Before I go to sleep,
I will lock all the doors.
I will lock myself in.

Goodbye, Goodbye

I haven't been this sad
since someone died.
Going away from you is about as easy
as waltzing out of my own body
and never coming back.
We have always been happy.
No one wants to be sad.
I could get so desperate
for some happy solution
I might drink the bottle of Joy
over by the sink,
and blow huge, delicate bubbles
out of my mouth for hours
so we could die laughing.
If you act happy, then you are happy,
I tell myself, trying to salvage my life
as a relatively slow-paced comedy,
though each minute it threatens
to degenerate into
a painfully lugubrious soap opera.
Meanwhile my art is becoming
a convalescent home
for the perennially brokenhearted.

Like right now, I am locked in my cabin
trying to say goodbye,
but writing this poem
as if my life depended on it,
and it does.

Leopards

Leopards break into the temple and drink to the dregs what is in the sacrificial pitchers; this is repeated over and over again; finally it can be calculated in advance, and it becomes part of the ceremony.

–Kafka

The ceremony of your life is dull,
each day the same, old, boring ritual.

Surprise yourself and let the fun begin.
Open the door and let the leopards in.

Lolita

Lemme read your dirty book, man!
Damn! It's God-damn Litachure!!

−from the introduction to The Annotated Lolita, by Alfred Appel, Jr.

Vladimir Nabokov authored a blockbuster.

Beautiful nymphet's abused by a cad.

Most of the novel is boring and sad.

Readers expecting some steamy pornography,

closing the book, might suspect they've been had.

In The Small Town Of Claremont, As Summer Begins To Turn Into Autumn, The Apprentice Finally Gets To Meet The Master, And Composes These Simple Quatrains In Admiration and Gratitude

For Bob Mezey

If you can find some pleasure in my lines,

and laugh out loud, or maybe shed some tears,

you should, with Justice, feel a little proud.

You have been teaching me for many years.

I have often come to your poems for my mind's pleasure,

for lessons in the art of rhyme and measure,

and I have tried to write as well as you.

Few poets can. I still have work to do.

John Ashbery

His words can flash and dazzle, cast a spell.

He had nothing to say, but said it well.

On The Physical Shape Of Poems

I like poems that are thin,
that stand in a corner of the page,
quiet, self-effacing.
And I like larger poems
that can take command of the page,
like sonnets or sestinas,
magisterial.

But sometimes a poem squats
on the page likes a huge frog.
How your blood runs cold
when the poem is your dark lady
and you try everything
and you cannot get her out.

The Poem About The Hungarians

I stayed up late last night,
reading and writing poems.
When I came to bed,
you were asleep, but you said:
Did you finish it,
the poem about the Hungarians?
I laughed. You must have been dreaming.

When I woke up this morning,
your dream began to haunt me.
I know I am being followed
by the poem about the Hungarians.
It wants me to write it down.
It will not leave me alone.

I don't know anything
about Hungary. I remember
a photograph from a newspaper:
a street full of Russian tanks.

I think of a gypsy wedding.
One of the gypsies smiles.
You can see the bride and the groom
dance in his gold tooth.

I think of black forests,
a castle on a mountain,
the moon, like an evil lamp,
hiding behind the clouds.

Who will ever tell you
the poem about the Hungarians?

It will probably haunt me forever,
like a really good dream
you might have had last night,
a dream you can never remember.

The Music That There Is

He would spend a long time
preparing the instruments
for the grand symphony

when the music that there is
would desire to hear itself
and start the bows moving

across the perfect strings,
give breath to the woodwinds and horns,
send batons down to the drums,

except that the music is deaf
and untroubled by desire,
the instruments would never suffice.

Already he detects
squeaks in the highest ranges,
a hollowness in the percussion,

an uncorrectable,
disturbing tendency
towards a pervasive flatness.

And the only music he gets
is that of his own desire
(mutilated so?)

for that other music
which has no desire
and can never be written.

Rivers

The Nile, the Amazon, the Mississippi,
the Congo, the Colorado, the Rio Grande.
The names of rivers conjure up the rivers
and they come alive in my imagination.
One day, years ago, in New Orleans,
I stood on a hill overlooking the Mississippi
and watched the river rolling toward the Gulf.
Where the hell did all this water come from?
I knew that every river has its headwaters
and tributaries that feed it along its course,
although the might and majesty of the river
made its origin seem a mystery.
I watched the river and was thrilled with wonder.

Where are the headwaters of poetry?
No one will ever find them. They are hidden
somewhere in the heart or in the soul,
with the uncanny power to conceive
the river of words flowing down the page
into the deep ocean of the mind.

Wife

In Pittsburgh,
she remembers Mississippi,
the dead roses.

She tells me her dreams
and they frighten me.
I love her for that.

Night comes.
There is a full moon.
My wife lights her candles.

You Might Know Everything

You might know everything there is to know.

You might win lots of money on some quiz show.

But this is not enough. There's something wrong.

You know the words, the tune, but not the song.

What I Remember

Charles Baudelaire knew that the human heart
Associates with not the whole but part.
The parts are fetishes, invariable
Particularities that furnish Hell.
Thom Gunn

There was a young lady called Linda,

or maybe her name was Belinda.

There's been so many dames;

I have trouble with names,

but I'll never forget her pudenda.

Talking About Divorce

I was talking with some friends tonight.
Michael said his wife had filed for divorce
and he was suffering with grief and fear.
I told him I could understand his pain,
that my first divorce carved a deep wound in my soul.
"It was my first adult experience
of serious failure and of frightening loss.
I'm not certain the wound has ever healed
under all the bandages of Time."
He asked if my second divorce was also painful.
"No," I said, "I was happy and relieved.
It had to happen, and I have no regrets."
Michael thought a while and then he said,
"Glad to hear it. I'll look forward to my next one."

Closer And Closer Approximations

I never told you I loved you nearly enough.

I never loved you nearly enough.

I never loved you.

For Theresa

So maybe God didn't create the world
so that billions of years later I could touch your face
and tell you I love you, but that is how it feels.

The Fifth Step

AA 5th Step: *Admitted to God, to ourselves, and to another human being the exact nature of our wrongs*

I go to AA meetings every morning.
They've helped me to stay sober a long time.
At this morning's meeting, someone told a story
I had never heard before, about a man
meeting his sponsor one day to do his 5th Step.
After the meeting was over, I heard that this story
had been told in AA meetings for several years.
The man, a sober alcoholic, is anxious
because he knows he will confess today
a terrible thing he'd done when he was drinking.
Feeling guilty and ashamed, he finally admits:
"Once, when I was drunk, I fucked a chicken."
His sponsor smiles, and says, "Did yours die too?"

So, Is Bestiality Big In Blythe?

Said a dirty old shepherd called Bruno,
There is one thing that I do know.
A woman is fine, a sheep is divine,
But a llama is numero uno.

Daniel was talking to his friends one night.
He told us he had never met a woman
that he could date, during the last two years
while he's been living and working up in Blythe.
Women there are scarce and hard to find.
If you're looking for a girlfriend or a wife,
odds are you won't get lucky up in Blythe.
A wise-ass Muse inspired me to say,
So, is bestiality big in Blythe?
I laughed, not just because the line seemed funny,
but because it surprised me and delighted me.
I loved the way it sounded, the percussive
alliteration of the labials,
and I wanted to preserve it in a poem.

Good things astonishing and beautiful
come from some hidden well in the universe,
once in a while, as unexpected gifts,
like a line of poetry, like love.

Daniel's a good man. I know one day
some woman will astonish him with love.

Meanwhile, you have to take what you can get.
Say you're walking down a country road,
and a pretty, little llama waltzes by...

Sorry Daniel, I'm just trying to be funny,
and I simply wanted another chance to say,
So, is bestiality big in Blythe?

The World

The words of philosophers litter history.
The world is a metaphor for mystery.

About The Author

Michael Creagan, the oldest of seven children, grew up in New Haven and Hamden, Connecticut. He graduated in 1970 from the University of Pittsburgh School of Medicine, and has been working as a doctor ever since. For the past 46 years, he has worked as an emergency medicine specialist in Southern California. Twice married and twice divorced, he lives in Upland, California with his dog, Belle.

Acknowledgements

These poems have been published in The National Review

    Heart Attack

    In The Hospital, Watching People Die

    A Grave Poem For A Gift

    No One Should Write About Things Like This

    Night

    Taking A Walk On Sunday

    Hotel

    A Brief Inferno

    Jacarandas

    Road Kill

    Telephone Greeting

    Prayer

    At Benjamin Pond

    Old Words

Poems in the Susquehanna Quarterly

    Taking A Walk On Sunday

    Hotel

    Looking For Metaphors In The Mountains

Poems In The Claremont Courier

> Poem Smoking A Cigarette in A Dark Corner Of The Page
>
> After A Book Of Old Chinese Poetry, I Stay Awake Tonight And Write This Poem

Lyric Magazine

> Another Riddle
> —a different version, with a different title

Poems Of The American West, An Anthology of poetry, edited by Robert Mezey

> Taking A Walk On Sunday

Four Poets, an anthology of poetry published by St. Vincent College Press

> In The Hospital, Watching People Die
> Alba